87 575

769.56
S
Schwarz
    Beginners' guide to stamp
collecting

DATE DUE			
AUG 1 6 1996			

Beginner's Guide to Stamp Collecting

TED SCHWARZ

ARCO PUBLISHING, INC.
NEW YORK

Published by Arco Publishing, Inc.
215 Park Avenue South, New York, N.Y. 10003

Library of Congress Cataloging in Publication Data

Schwarz, Ted, 1945-
  Beginner's guide to stamp collecting.

  Includes index.
  1. Postage-stamps—Collectors and collecting—
Handbooks, manuals, etc. I. Title.
HE6215.S3   1983   769.56 '075   83-9956
ISBN 0-668-05547-2   (Cloth)

Printed in the United States of America

10   9   8   7   6   5   4   3   2   1

Contents

Acknowledgments

Special thanks go to Jeanne Mears at *Linn's Stamp Monthly* and to *Linn's* publisher, Amos Press, for providing the photographs used in this book. I also am grateful to John Birkinbine II, of American Philatelic Brokers in Tucson, Arizona, for his encouragement and assistance.

Introduction

They may not look like much, those colorful bits of paper that move the mail. Yet stamps can open a world more exciting than television or the movies. They can reflect your love of sports or the excitement of the Old West. Do you like dancing? The excitement of space travel? How about boxing, karate, delicate flowers, exotic fish, or fast race cars? No matter what your personal interest, postage stamps can help you enjoy it more. And as your interests change, you can reflect them in the stamps you collect.

You can begin collecting postage stamps at any age. Chances are, if you go to school, you may find collectors as young as seven or eight. At the other extreme are collectors who did not begin saving stamps until they were grandparents, retired from their jobs. Major league athletes have collected stamps, as have presidents of the United States and the crowned heads of Europe. Beautiful collections have been obtained at no greater expense than a small portion of a collector's allowance or money earned from a paper route. Wealthy adults may spend large sums for their collections, yet the size and pleasure of their philatelic holdings will be no greater than your own. Young or old, rich or poor, in school or out, everyone can enjoy this special hobby.

The designs of postage stamps are meant to reflect the world we live in. Are you excited by the Old West? You can share the excitement of gold and silver exploration with the 4-cent stamp issued in 1959 to honor the pioneer silver miners. You can feel the excitement of the Pony Express rider racing across the continent, fleeing from pursuing Indians and marauding badmen on the 3-cent stamp of 1940 and the 4-cent stamp of 1960 (commemorating the hundredth anniversary of the Pony Express). The colorful Conestoga wagon, the cowboy's version of today's motor home, was found on the U.S. Utah centennial 3-cent stamp of 1947.

Souvenir sheets issued by Sierra Leone in honor of the wedding of Prince Charles and Lady Diana.

Or perhaps you're interested in space travel. You can share the excitement of the early astronauts who left their spacecraft and walked literally out of this world with the 1967 twin 5-cent stamps (called a se-tenant pair) honoring the *Gemini 4* space walk. The historic docking of the *Apollo* and Russian *Soyuz* spacecraft of 1975 can be enjoyed on 10-cent stamps issued in July of that year. And the early moon landing was commemorated in 1969 when the American astronauts took their first steps where man had never gone before; the stamp issued was a 6-cent *Apollo 8* mission stamp that depicts the rising earth over the lunar surface.

If your interest is real-life fairy-tale romances, you can trace the marriage of Prince Charles and Lady Diana on the Great Britain stamps of 1981. Their baby, the future king of England, had his birth commemorated the following year. Even earlier British stamps were issued honoring the marriage of Princess Anne and Mark Phillips (1973) and the twenty-fifth wedding anniversary of Queen Mother Elizabeth and King George VI (1948), parents of the present queen. The love story of King Edward VIII who abandoned the throne for the American woman he loved is remembered on the 1936 ½ pence (½d) stamps of Great Britain.

Or you might be interested in athletics. Canada highlighted pole vaulting on a 1975 20-cent Olympic issue and hurdling on a 50-cent issue that same year. Swimming was honored on an 8 + 2

cent semi-postal stamp in 1974 and a similar denomination honored fencing the following year.

Many adults find pleasure in the paintings of the Great Masters. They enjoy the idea of being able to travel to museums to see the various masterpieces which hang there. Unfortunately they may not live very close to such museums or they may not be able to afford extensive travel. For them, the ideal topical collection might consist of masterpieces in miniature—paintings reproduced on the postage stamps of the world.

Stamp collectors seem to know more than the average person. Wars and revolutions cause the boundaries and names of countries to change every few years. Each time someone new comes to power or countries are captured by their enemies, different stamps are issued. Collectors are among the first to learn of these changes and the names and the people in power. The average person may take months to acquire the knowledge the collector has gained by studying the new stamps.

This book will show you how to plan, organize, find, and buy and sell your stamps. You will also learn postal history, a four-thousand-year-old story that is colorful and fascinating and adds yet another dimension to your new hobby.

1

Getting Started in Stamp Collecting

Stamp collecting is one of the least expensive hobbies to begin. The cost can be as low as just saving the stamps on the envelopes you receive through the mail. You can ask family members, neighbors, friends and/or business associates to save envelopes for you so that you can check the stamps. They can be stored in envelopes, shoeboxes, or almost any other way you desire. However, you probably will want to have a few basic tools for building a collection that you can enjoy for years to come.

THE TOOLS OF A STAMP COLLECTOR

Aside from stamps, you will need tongs, hinges, and an album. Tongs are like flat-bladed tweezers. They are used to examine and mount stamps without risking getting fingerprints on the paper or otherwise damaging them.

Stamp hinges are specially designed adhesive attachments meant for mounting your stamps in an album. The hinges will not damage the stamp in any way. They are peelable when dry and are the least expensive method for safely mounting them. The cost is only a few cents for a package of hundreds.

UNDER NO CIRCUMSTANCES SHOULD YOU MOUNT A POSTAGE STAMP WITH ADHESIVE TAPE OF ANY TYPE. USE ONLY SPECIALLY MADE STAMP HINGES. OTHERWISE THE STAMPS WILL BE DAMAGED AND RENDERED WORTHLESS.

There are all kinds of albums, a general world album often being most desirable for the beginning collector with no immedi-

ate special interest. You can build a collection of different types of stamps, deciding which ones you like best. Then you can buy a specialized album for just one country or a topical album to hold a collection built around one theme—such as art stamps issued by the countries of the world.

A magnifying glass is an optional extra. However, it is a great help in studying and identifying your stamps.

Eventually you will also want to own a stamp catalog, a guide

This issue, which had a color error, is popular with collectors.

that provides a listing of all the stamps issued by a country, their descriptions, their current prices (mint and used), their pictures and, often, information concerning overprints, known errors and rarities, and other unusual variations you might encounter. A number of companies issue such catalogs, the two best known coming from the Scott Publishing Company and the Minkus Publishing Company. Scott publishes several volumes of catalogs and they are updated each year. Each stamp has a special "Scott" number code assigned to it and this code is used by the majority of dealers and album manufacturers to designate the different stamps. Minkus also has a numbering system, but this system is used by fewer dealers and collectors. However, all other information pertaining to the stamp will be identical, although the value of the stamp may vary.

Catalogs are also available from some of the larger stamp dealers, such as the H. E. Harris & Co. of Massachusetts, which does a large volume of direct-mail selling to collectors. All the catalogs can be purchased at local stamp shops and in certain bookstores as well, or they may be borrowed from the public library. As long as you are having no trouble studying your stamps and finding the appropriate location in your album, the purchase of a catalog is not essential.

TYPES OF COLLECTIONS AND STAMPS

The simplest collection is a general stamp collection. You collect stamps of the world or the stamps of one particular country. You seek everything available within your price range. Usually you will have to buy the older stamps, although many of these may be expensive. Few collectors are ever able to *complete* their collections of the United States, Great Britain, Canada, and other older countries that have been issuing stamps almost since they were first invented. Even fewer collectors have even considered completing such a collection since great cost would be involved. However, thousands of stamps can be obtained, sorted by country and mounted, at relatively little expense, so a large collection can be both fun and a never-ending project.

Some collectors like to select only the newer countries and

New countries provide a collecting area difficult to handle with traditional albums. In this case, Antigua and Barbuda gained independence only recently, so the earliest stamps of independence are too few in number for their own album. Such stamps rightfully belong in a stock book until you obtain pages for the new country. You might choose to make your own pages for all future issues or wait until the countries are included in the supplemental pages sold for postal albums of the world.

stamp issuing organizations such as the United Nations. It is possible to obtain complete collections of their issues without paying hundreds of dollars per stamp as is the case with the rarities of other nations.

Topical collections can be assembled using an album that has blank pages. You design your own layout and mount the stamps as you choose. For example, suppose you specialize in stamps featuring paintings. You might arrange your collection so that the pages are divided according to the countries that issue the stamps. Or you might decide to learn which of the world's museums have

the various paintings in their collections. Then you would use one or more blank pages to represent the Prado, the Louvre, the Metropolitan, the Hermitage, and the other great museums of the world. The stamps would be mounted so that the paintings represented on them would be "hung" in their appropriate museums. There are also topical albums available from companies such as White Ace that give you already prepared pages to mount your stamps on.

Some people like to expand their collection beyond the topical theme. They collect not only the stamps but related material. Thus a collection of postage stamps issued by the Confederate States during the Civil War might be combined with a collection of books about that period. The same collector might have old tokens, coins, perhaps uniform items, and other material. The stamp collection is one part of a larger holding all related to the same theme.

Sports, for both the disabled and the physically fit, is always a popular topic. These inexpensive stamps are typical of what might be included in a sports collection. More-valuable stamps also can be added.

Another approach is to only collect items of postal origin related to a particular topical theme. A collection of stamps revolving around a medical theme might also include envelopes with special medical office or hospital postage meter labels. There might be First Day Covers (envelopes, often carrying an artistic design in one corner, with a postage stamp canceled on the first day it is issued) with the medical theme, and perhaps envelopes autographed by medical personnel related to the topic shown on the stamp.

Some collectors like to acquire plate blocks or regular blocks

These Togolese stamps commemorating the handicapped can be mounted with little concern for saving the adhesive on the back. Most contemporary issues appear in such a quantity that hinging is perfectly acceptable.

of stamps. A block of stamps usually comprises from four to six stamps in a rectangular pattern. These stamps are generally the same design, although in some instances it may take several different designs to make a block. For example, when the United States issued a sheet of stamps showing the state flags of all 50 states, an entire sheet made up the block. The sheet comprised the 50 different stamps, so a full sheet was desired by the block collector. A few years earlier, a two-stamp design was issued by the United States to commemorate the first walk in space. One stamp showed the space ship and a cord which, when the adjoining stamp was attached, had the cord connected to an astronaut. The two stamps made one design and a block, which consisted of four stamps, would actually have only two different sets.

A plate block is the block of stamps that includes the plate number found in one or more corners of the sheet. Because there is generally just one plate block per sheet, it is much more difficult to put together a collection of plate blocks than it is to assemble a collection of regular blocks. Thus they are more highly prized by collectors and generally command a substantial premium.

There are albums for collectors of plate blocks for certain countries, including the United States. These are most desired when in "Mint" condition—the way in which they come from the Post Office: unhinged, with original gum, and uncanceled. Older scarce and rare plate blocks are quite expensive since the value is four times the value of the single stamp plus an extra percentage for the plate number being attached. It is difficult to find used plate blocks or regular blocks because most people use a single postage stamp or two or three stamps of different denominations for their mail.

First Day Covers (FDC's), mentioned earlier, can form a collection by themselves. This involves collecting the entire envelope with a stamp that is canceled on the first day of issue. Most collectors want what are known as cacheted First Day Covers. These are covers with a drawing or photograph in the left-hand corner or some other location which can be readily seen. There are many companies that sell First Day Covers and you can pay from a dollar to many, many dollars for special silk cacheted covers.

Philatelic/Numismatic Covers (PNC's) combine both a stamp and a related coin or medal. During the American Bicentennial Celebration period of 1973–1976, the U.S. Post Office created special First Day PNC's which had a stamp related to the

Whereas many countries—for example, the United States—feature primarily historical figures in commemoratives, other countries may also feature popular personalities. Shown in the illustration are stamps issued by Jamaica after the death of Bob Marley, the Jamaican Reggae musician/folk hero.

American Revolution and/or Colonial era and a medal representing that same time. There were four different designs of that issue. The majority of PNC's however, are made by private companies.

There was a time when some collectors purchased a complete

sheet of stamps for each new issue from the Post Office. This is expensive because of the high face value, and such sheets seldom have much resale interest. Dealers who buy them, unless the stamps are unusual for some reason, will usually break them up, selling plate blocks, blocks, and singles from each sheet. The exceptions are special issues, such as the 50 state flags or the 50 state birds issued by the United States Post Office in which a full sheet is necessary to obtain one of each issue.

The main stamps collected by most hobbyists are commem-

Typical of topical stamps are these from Togo, commemorating feats of space exploration by both Russians and Americans.

oratives and regular issues. Regular-issue (or definitive) stamps are stamps meant to serve postal needs for a long period of time. The first stamps introduced in England, the United States, Canada, and many other countries were regular issues. They usually had the image of one of the nation's leaders and were not meant to be replaced until a change in the postal rates took place.

Commemoratives, such as the Columbian Exposition stamps introduced in the United States in 1893, relate to a specific event; others, such as the 3-cent stamp issued in 1956 to mark Benjamin Franklin's 250th birthday, honor an anniversary. They are issued for a short period of time in order to remind the public of either a period of history or the accomplishments of one or more individuals. The Columbian Exposition stamps, for example, show various scenes relating to Columbus' discovery of America and his dealings with Queen Isabella of Spain.

Commemorative stamps are generally more colorful and varied in the art than regular issues. They are also larger to allow for the quality of the art.

Souvenir sheets are another philatelic device that are quite popular. These and miniature sheets are often issued in conjunc-

Souvenir sheet issued by Antigua.

tion with a philatelic exhibition or convention. They may have several tiny stamps on an oversized piece of paper. Sometimes a sheet is meant to be mounted on an album page. These are designed around a theme and may reproduce a work of art, such as a Chagall Window souvenir sheet issued by the United Nations Postal Administration. This was a reproduction of Marc Chagall's Stained Glass Memorial Window located in UN Head-quarters in New York. This particular miniature sheet was printed in 1967 and, though it could be used for mailing, was actually meant specifically for collectors.

Buying and collecting miniature and souvenir sheets is very different from buying sheets of regular postage stamps. In the United States, stamps are usually printed in sheets of 50 to 100, depending upon their size; they are also available in rolls (coils), vending machine booklets, and in other forms. There was a time when collectors bought whole sheets and placed them in albums; some even continue this practice today. However, these common sheets of stamps have little resale value and are not worth collect-ing as a beginner.

Souvenir cards are philatelic issues usually meant to com-memorate a particular international philatelic exhibition. They have been issued since 1960, although souvenir cards dating back to 1938 exist. The latter was meant to accompany a special Phila-telic Truck which toured the United States during the period from 1939 to 1941. The cost of a card is low at the time of its release, but because many of the earlier cards were issued in very small quantities (10,391 in the case of the card for the First Inter-national Philatelic Congress in Barcelona, Spain, March 26, 1960), the early issues command substantial prices.

The maximum card is a European specialty whose popularity has spread to Asia and the United States. It is a postcard which has a picture which corresponds to the design of a postage stamp: the stamp should be stuck to the picture side of the postcard and canceled with an appropriate postmark linking the theme of the stamp and the postcard. This is usually different from the spe-cially designed card/stamp combinations offered by the Chinese postal service. Instead an attempt is made to match the scenes with what may be somewhat unrelated images. One example is a postcard showing a judo throw combined with a stamp meant for the Olympics, which also showed two men practicing a judo throw. One scene was not taken directly from the other but they both show the same type of image.

The United States Postal Service offers souvenir sheets that have an engraving, the story behind a commemorative issue and the stamps, themselves canceled on the First Day of Issue. These are approximately the size of a standard notebook page and are an unusual way to obtain new stamps. The total philatelic issue becomes the collectible rather than just the postage stamp.

Souvenir sheets are issued infrequently by the United States, Canada, and other large countries. However, they are a regular part of the issues of smaller countries, which use the sale of stamps to collectors as a way of earning extra money. Many small countries rely on the collector purchase of commemorative stamps, souvenir sheets, and similar items to help pay for the running of the government. These are often sold at a rather high price because they can be used to pay postage. However, since they are meant to raise revenue rather than service mail, they are not likely to maintain a value equal even to their original cost. Most collectors and dealers will pay very little for them on the resale market. The stamps of the ''Sand Dune'' countries of the Middle East are one such example. If you enjoy them, you are best off buying them a year or two after they are issued when the price will be relatively low.

The most elaborate ''stamp'' or ''souvenir sheet'' ever issued was a record produced by the country of Bhutan, a country discussed in Chapter 9. That record could actually be played yet was used to send the mail.

Special stamps, such as those used to indicate the payment of a tax on newspapers, magazines, and similar materials, are also collected by some individuals. These are a part of the social history of a country, especially revenue stamps, yet usually have little or no artwork. Often these are known as ''back-of-the-book'' issues, since most albums place these stamps at the back, concentrating on regular issues, commemoratives, and air mail and special delivery stamps at the front.

One special stamp that is both artistic and highly prized is the Duck or hunting permit stamp. Duck stamps are used for hunting licenses and are inscribed ''Department of Interior.'' The stamp is proof of payment for the license and is designed with as much concern for quality art as a commemorative issue. Not only do collectors take pride in acquiring the American duck stamps, they also bid on the original painting created for the design. The artist's work is routinely sold for several thousand dollars.

NED GREEN, STAMP COLLECTOR

Stamp collectors come in many sizes and shapes. Age, sex, occupation, education, and other factors have nothing to do with enjoying stamp collecting as a hobby. There is something for everyone in this unique pastime.

Most collectors take quiet pleasure in their stamps, visiting dealers and stamp shows, perhaps belonging to philatelic clubs, yet generally not becoming well known for their interest. One outstanding exception was Ned Green.

Green was one of the most eccentric individuals ever to appear on Nassau Street, New York's center for stamp dealers during the first half of this century. Although not particularly knowledgeable, he was certainly the most flamboyant and enthusiastic character on the scene.

E.H. (Ned) Green, nicknamed the "Colonel," spent money as if he owned a mint, buying yachts, private railroad cars, rare coins, and diamonds. He also bought postage stamps in a manner unlike any collector before or since.

Ned knew nothing about stamps when he walked into a New York City stamp dealer's shop in the early 1900's. He asked to see a collection of stamps and the clerk showed him an envelope containing a small mixture. This was a typical packet of the day, the same approach to starting a collection that you might use today.

Ned Green was not like you or me. He asked the clerk to keep bringing forth larger and larger quantities until the clerk showed Green a package of a few thousand stamps selling for around a hundred dollars. This would have been a major purchase for a beginner with money, but Ned Green was more than that. He was an eccentric whose preconceived notions about the hobby were not to be thwarted by reality.

Green knew a "real" collection costs thousands of dollars and he was carrying a wad of new one-hundred-dollar bills to pay for it. If the clerk wouldn't treat him fairly, he would go somewhere else.

Green went to the next dealer on the street. For some reason he tolerated the normal business approach this time, buying a small packet of stamps and a basic album which he claimed was for the son of his laundryman. A few days later he returned to the store where he made his purchase and bought his first "real" collection—a collector's multi-volume accumulation that had been consigned to the dealer. The price was $31,000 and Ned paid cash.

Green was a contradiction in the world of philately. He educated himself enough to understand the value of certain issues, yet he never attempted to learn the scope of the field. In most areas he had far less knowledge than you will have when you finish reading this book.

For example, Willard Snyder, a Philadelphia, Pennsylvania, stamp dealer, was quoted concerning Green in the book *The Day They Shook the Plum Tree*. He said: "On May 13, 1918, a young man named W. T. Robey came into the New York Avenue branch of the Washington, D.C., post office to buy some air mail stamps. A clerk pulled out a sheet of stamps and handed it to Robey, who in turn gave the clerk twenty-four dollars, the cost of the hundred stamps.

"Almost simultaneously the clerk, who knew a great deal about stamps, and Robey, who knew enough, noticed something was amiss with these. The clerk made a grab for them, but the customer was quicker and jerked them away. He said he'd paid for them, refused to give them up, and walked out of the building.

"As soon as Robey got around the corner he looked at his buy and discovered that the plane in the center was upside down.

One of America's most expensive issues—the 24-cent airmail invert depicting a Curtis Jenny biplane. Ned Green bought a sheet of these in 1918 for $20,000. Today, just one of these stamps is worth considerably more than the lot was back then.

He must have felt like the guy who discovered the Comstock Lode. At the time nobody knew how many of these irregular stamps were in circulation, but dealers believed there couldn't have been many because the error was obvious: It was a first run, and they had just been put on sale.

"As it turned out there were only four hundred and they never should have left the Government Printing Office. We don't know what happened to the other three sheets but we do know the history of Robey's buy. Robey, acting on the advice of Percy McGraw Mann, then an Eastern philatelist and publisher, sold the set to Eugene Klein, a Philadelphia dealer, for fifteen thousand dollars. That was a neat profit for Robey and must have started a million kids collecting stamps.

"Colonel Green heard about the stamps and offered Klein a fast two-thousand-dollar profit. Klein held out for three thousand dollars more and sold the stamps to Green, on May 21, 1918, for twenty thousand dollars. The Colonel took out the choice 'positions' from the sheet and hung on to them for years. He made a smart move when he decided to sell his stamps individually. By doing this he created a market where none existed.

"He kept the prime positions, including the center line block. These were the most valuable. He numbered every one of the stamps lightly in pencil on the back so that a buyer would know the exact position his stamp held on the set. This is important to philatelists. The Colonel now had for disposal nineteen straight-edge stamps and the rest with perforations. Perforations make a stamp worth more. He put them on the market and they were grabbed up so fast it would take your breath away."

But Green was ignorant in some ways, too. He once bought the Joseph Leavy specialty collection of Belgium stamps including re-entries and plate varieties carefully described on the pages along with plate positions. Green had a crew of women cataloging his collection and he had one woman remove all the stamps, separate the "duplicates," and throw the pages away. A lifetime study was destroyed, though the stamps, themselves, remained unharmed.

Green was regularly cheated by stamp dealers in New York. They learned that the "Colonel" was so rich he would buy a collection at an exorbitant price to get a few stamps he needed. Thus one store owner had clerks take a few days filling in an album with junk material that had not been selling. In addition they placed quality United States material that they knew Ned needed in with the junk. The quality material was worth approximately $7,000 to $8,000 in catalog value, but the thousands of other stamps in the album might altogether bring just a few hundred dollars. The album pages containing the good material were slightly marked so the dealer who showed Green the stamps could casually flip through the album, revealing only the good material. He gave the impression that no matter which page he might turn to, the stamps would be good ones.

Green was fooled by the doctored album. He believed the dealer's story that the collection had belonged to a Russian noble and bartered the price down from $25,000 to $21,000. He left thinking he had gotten a bargain.

Green's purchase was not unusual. He spent as much as $77,000 in an afternoon when buying stamps, and acquisitions of $10,000 to $25,000 were normal for him.

After Green's death, a property inventory was taken. The official appraisal of the stamps set the Green Collection at $1,298,444. However, it is believed that the figure was deliberately kept quite *low* to help avoid taxes.

2

Sources of Stamps

The simplest way to begin your collection is to let people know you are interested in stamps. Ask businesses, friends, and family to save their stamps for you. Often you will find that when you tell people you are starting a stamp collection, they will give you collections long buried in their attics. Many times someone will collect stamps, then pass them on to a relative who has no interest in continuing the collection. That person does not want to throw them away and may have found that the stamps are common enough that there is no big money to be made by selling them to a dealer. The collection is simply stored and the current owner is delighted to give the stamps away to someone he or she knows will enjoy them.

Look around in your house or apartment for old letters and postcards, visit flea markets and antique or junk stores, and rummage with your friends through their basements and attics (if you are young, get your friends' parents' permission!).

The best part about obtaining older letters or even old collections is not the value of the stamps themselves, for most will be common issues, but rather the fact that the stamps will be hard to find today. The common stamps from the turn of the century, especially those from other countries, are not readily obtainable in quantity. They are not valuable, but there is so little demand for them in many communities that the only way you can obtain them is through the larger dealers. It is always more fun to acquire stamps in your home area than to have to purchase them mail order.

Once the mail has been delivered, most people have no interest in the stamps that helped it reach its destination. Envelopes and wrappings are discarded. These discards, saved from your own mail, from businesses, and even stamps found in flea markets on the backs of postcards or on envelopes can provide you with an excellent basis for your collection.

Save the stamps you get at home, including those sent to other family members. Often these will be current stamps and there may be many duplicates. However, you will find that even current stamps are eventually in great demand. Many collectors fail to save them, so they make great trading stamps in the future. These current stamps will be "historic" to collectors who begin five or ten years from now. Also, there is a broad range of current stamps. You will be receiving many different denominations in current use if you watch closely. Even "junk" mail has a treasure trove of nonprofit stamps, bulk-rate stamps, and similar material.

Talk with local business people who receive large quantities of mail; ask if they will save you their envelopes. Newspapers, banks, stores that sell by mail, and similar companies might be willing to cooperate. Often one person handles the mail and will toss envelopes and/or stamps into a bag for you. All the stamps will be attached to easily removed paper.

If you obtain postcards with stamps, especially older ones, you may want to save them instead of removing the stamps. Postcards, with their attractive scenes and often interesting notes scrawled on the back, can be a popular collectible. Many stamp collectors also collect postcards. Others trade the cards with the stamps for similar stamps already off paper. Any item of interest that has gone through the mail—and postcards certainly fit this category—can be more interesting than just the stamp alone.

More expensive stamps can be purchased individually, but the cheapest way to buy is in bulk. Packets of stamps are often available, with dozens or hundreds of inexpensive stamps sold according to the country of origin or a particular topic, such as stamps commemorating space travel. For more money, you can buy packets of world stamps containing thousands of different issues from many countries. Economy packets are usually available for prices ranging from less than a dollar to a hundred dollars or more for many thousands of stamps.

A variation of the packet is the "missionary mixture." Many overseas religious orders will take the stamps from envelopes they receive and place them in bags as received. There is no effort to avoid duplication or to sort the stamps. They are then sold by weight, a kilogram bag usually being the largest routinely available. This is an excellent way to obtain duplicates for trading, but

These stamps from Saint Lucia are representative of those found in packets. Although some of the stamps have large denominations, so many stamps were issued that they are not especially valuable.

Stamps like these from Togo are frequently found in packets. They are issued as commemoratives specifically to appeal to individuals who like either the country or the art but have a limited budget. Such stamps are well-centered and fully gummed.

you can not expect the variety found in other mixtures.

The stamps sold in packets and mixtures will either be on paper or off paper. Off-paper stamps are those that have been removed from envelopes or that were never sent through the mail, these can be either mint stamps or precancels. On-paper stamps are cut from envelopes, and you will have to soak the stamps and envelope corner in order to separate them. This is time-consuming, and must be done carefully in order not to damage the stamp.

THE POST OFFICE

Your local U.S. Post Office station is also a source for new stamps. The post offices of the world have learned that collectors should be encouraged. The new stamps you buy for your collection generate income without expense. Normally a postage stamp is purchased to pay the cost of moving a letter or package through the mail. Stamps that are not used for mail service provide bonus income for the government.

Many larger cities have a post office where there is a special philatelic window for collectors. You can buy commemoratives, regular issues, plate blocks, or stamp kits, or any other item of a philatelic nature if it is a current issue—postcards, postal envelopes, airletter sheets, etc. At the philatelic window you can take your time because there are no regular postal patrons behind you. The clerk will be glad to sell you a plate block or a Zip Code block from a sheet of stamps. And you also will be able to obtain information on ordering souvenir sheets and other collector items not normally sold over the counter.

In the Appendix, you will find information on countries that offer stamps by mail, from their philatelic services department. Send a self-addressed envelope to the desired country with an adequate number of International Reply Coupons for its return. This is the way dealers get most of their new issues and you can direct-order your stamps too, thereby avoiding the higher price dealers charge. The International Reply Coupon which you buy at your Post Office is like a country-to-country IOU that guarantees the person receiving it can exchange it for that country's postage of a quantity equal to the cost of the coupon. United States postage can carry a letter to Australia, for example, but U.S. postage is of no value on a letter originating in Australia and destined for the United States. Thus stamping the envelope will not result in its return. The coupon lets the Australian Post Office place adequate Australian postage on the envelope, collecting the postage money from the U.S. Post Office (which honors the coupon you purchase).

TRADING

Many collectors like to trade their stamps. Sometimes this is done by mailing the new issues from the country in which you live to pen pals in other nations, who exchange their new issues for yours. At other times, stamps are traded from collections at club meetings and among friends.

Here are some organizations that can help you make friends with other stamp collectors:

International Federation of Organizations for School Correspondence and Exchange (FIOCES), 29 rue D'Ulm, F-75005, Paris, France. Although this is primarily for students, younger adults around college age should investigate.

International Friendship League, 22 Batterymarch Street, Boston, Massachusetts 02109. This is a group supplying pen pals no matter what your age or interest.

League of Friendship, P.O. Box 509, Mt. Vernon, Ohio 43050. This is a limited organization that caters to pen pals primarily from 12 through 22. Again, contact them because age may not matter. Also remember that you may be making a lifelong friend abroad through such a group, so the rewards are often far greater than access to postage stamps different from your own.

Letters Abroad, 209 East 56th Street, New York, New York 10022. This group is interested in getting pen pals for anyone 16 and over. It is strongest in adult groups.

Student Letter Exchange, R.F.D. No. 4, Waseca, Minnesota 56093. This is only a student group for children from 10 through their late teens.

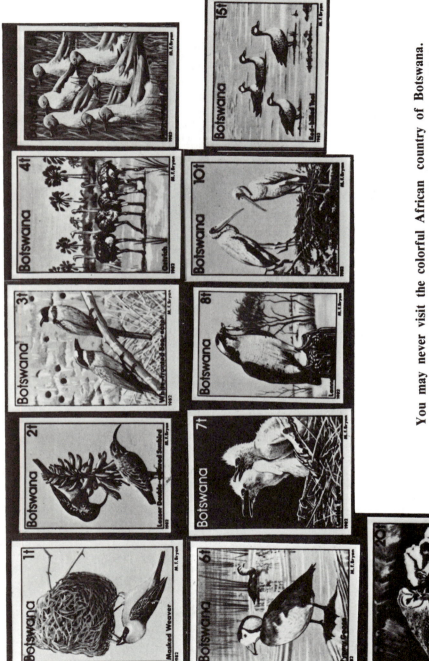

You may never visit the colorful African country of Botswana. However, a penpal can send you stamps of his or her country and help you to better understand that country, its people, and its history.

Stamps such as these from Guernsey are best purchased in a collection or obtained from a pen pal.

Voicespondence Club, c/o Robert Woodworth, 2904 State Hill Road, Unit F10, Wyomissing, Pennsylvania 19610. This organization is meant to provide voice communication among the blind and handicapped. If you are handicapped or know someone who is blind, you might combine your interests, since the tapes are sent through the mail. Most of the people will not be able to help since the majority are not sighted. However, since the handicapped other than the blind participate, it is a club to consider if you fit the membership requirements.

World Pen Pals, 1690 Como Avenue, St. Paul, Minnesota, 55108. This organization normally works with students in the 12- to 20-year age range.

Worldwide Tapetalk, 35 The Gardens, West Harrow, Middlesex, Hal 4HE, England. This is a club for all ages and will exchange tapes as well as letters, but it is not a club for the handicapped, although handicapped persons can join. Thus if your interest extends to voice as well, it is a good organization to join.

APPROVALS

Many magazines advertise stamps sold "on approval," usually to adults only. Approvals are packets of stamps selling for various prices, the total cost of which is relatively low. You select any of the stamps you want, then return the rest along with payment for your purchase.

Usually approvals are sold with a "come-on" either in the form of free stamps or stamps sold well below their normal cost. When you order this "special," you are also sent dozens to hundreds of stamps in packets, sorted by country or topic, from which to choose.

The cost of approvals is generally higher than you would pay a local dealer for the same items. However, they are an extremely convenient way to buy and give collectors in smaller communities access to stamps they might otherwise not readily find.

A person with excellent credit may be able to become part of an approval service that includes more expensive stamps. Scarce and rare issues, often worth many dollars or hundreds of dollars, will be sent. This is done once you have proven your honesty, because, until then, there is a chance that the stamps would be "lost" or otherwise not returned. Most approvals are relatively worthless despite their selling price. However, your purchases and your returning them promptly with the proper charge will make the dealer willing to cooperate.

There are also specialized approval services that only deal in the "better" or "rarer" issues, selling stamps that should prove good investments for the future. Many people are investing in stamps as a hedge against inflation as well as for the joy of assembling a collection. You, too, may be able to buy relatively inexpensive stamps that will increase in value rapidly over the next few years.

DEALERS

Buying from a reputable, established stamp dealer is always the best way to purchase stamps. You can order by mail, although much of the fun comes from being able to look through the dealer's stock and learn from his or her knowledge. You will be able to see and to choose from a wider range of stamps of the world and special topical collections than would be possible in any other way.

The larger your purchase, the more the honesty and knowledge of a dealer become a concern. Stamps are counterfeited, especially those that can be sold for a few hundred dollars or more. This is not a major problem unless you are the victim. A knowledgeable dealer will not only be able to spot many counterfeits, he will also arrange to have the stamps checked by nationally respected experts before the sale is final.

Select a stamp dealer with care, especially if you plan to become serious about the hobby in the years ahead. The dealer should have a wide selection of material and be an enthusiastic booster of stamp collecting. There should be books and catalogs available for you to study and/or purchase. The dealer also should be a member and promoter of both local stamp clubs and the national organization for collectors, known as the American Philatelic Society (APS). There is a second organization, almost as well known, called the Society of Philatelic Americans (SPA) and membership in that is a plus. In addition, if the dealer's stock has high enough value, he or she has been in business for a certain number of years, the dealer's reputation is high and he or she agrees to meet prescribed ethical business practices, the dealer may be a member of the American Stamp Dealers' Association. ASDA requires members to meet strict criteria or they will be expelled. Many dealers are not eligible for membership because they have not been in business long enough or they do not have sufficient high-value stock. They are still excellent nonetheless. However, if a stamp dealer is in a position to join ASDA and he or she chooses to not join, I would be tempted to go elsewhere. There may or may not be a problem, but why risk the chance?

AUCTIONS

One of the great myths of philately is the "need" to buy at auction. All the "important" stamps are sold at auction, one "expert" will tell you. "You can be certain of the quality of stamps sold at auction" is another popular comment. "Rarities have greater value if you can say that they were purchased during a major dealer's auction sale" is another statement frequently heard.

Although it is true that auctions are fun, exciting, and an opportunity to see philatelic items that may never enter your local dealer's shop, the quality of the merchandise is no better or worse than you will encounter when purchasing stamps over the counter, and the "pedigree" of sales is no guarantee that a stamp is genuine. See Chapter 10 for more on auctions.

3

How to Evaluate Stamps

At first glance, a stamp seems to be little more than a piece of paper on which artwork in miniature has been reproduced. The paper is of relatively high quality because of the handling the stamp will receive in the mail. The printing is routinely excellent and the stamps have either been canceled or are in mint condition as they came from the Post Office. It would seem that there is no reason to be worried about subtle differences in appearance.

Unfortunately, the reality is that stamps and the equipment used to print them are all made by extremely fallible humans. Paper can have areas which are thinner than expected. The gum may be unevenly spread. The printing may be off-center or the perforations laid down in such a way that they result in uneven margins. So many variations in quality can occur that collectors pay a premium for the best printings.

PRICE

Stamp values are given according to certain catalogs. The most popular are the Scott catalogs, which are updated annually. Each stamp in a Scott Catalog has a letter and number code. The letter tells you whether it is a regular issue, air mail stamp, or some other type of issue. The number just tells you when it was released because each country starts with the number "1" for its first stamp and moves forward from there.

Almost all dealers follow the Scott listings. When a dealer advertises, he or she will supply the country or origin and the Scott number to allow you to check the corresponding stamp number in the catalog. The Minkus Catalog is also used by some dealers, but all collectors and dealers alike understand the terminology of the Scott listings.

The Scott Catalog prices are general guides. Few stamps sell for as much as their Scott listing. Also, the company puts a minimum value of a few cents on each stamp because they know that this will be the least a dealer can charge and make any profit. Thus a stamp selling for five cents may not be worth that much on resale after you buy it. The figure is just meant as a minimum guide for when you buy the stamp individually in a retail store.

Scott prices for rarities are usually too low. Most rarities move up in value enough in the course of a year that the Scott price is outdated almost upon publication of the catalog. The real value to the Scott guides is that they provide relative price information for a stamp. By studying the catalogs of the past few years, you can tell if stamps have steadily increased in value, fluctuated because of speculation, or even gone down. You can also spot the common stamps which cost a few cents when purchased individually and sell for perhaps a fraction of a cent each in packets.

The price of a stamp is determined by many factors. First is the issue price. Stamps meant for use in the postal system and not just for sale to collectors generally hold their face value. This becomes the minimum you will have to pay for a mint stamp. Naturally, if you buy new stamps through a dealer instead of directly from a post office, the cost will have the dealer's markup. He or she needs to add enough to the price to be able to meet overhead and make a profit. This may be only a few cents, but it is something.

Catalogs help to determine the price for a stamp. Stamps that are used and found in such abundance as to be worthless will still be listed as having a value of at least 3 or 4 cents in the various pricing guides. This is because dealers always need to make some markup and these few cents represent the minimum they must charge for even a worthless stamp in order to stay in business. Collectors may not be requesting these stamps and the dealers may not bother to stock them, but should a sale be made, some money must change hands or the dealer can not meet expenses. Thus the smallest values listed for stamps in guidebooks may be higher than the price the stamps are worth to collectors.

At the other extreme are the high-priced stamps, the great rarities which seldom appear for sale. A stamp which is so rare that it is only sold at auction will usually be listed with the price paid at the last auction sale. Other stamps, not quite so rare, may be sold privately as well as by auction. The price listed becomes an estimate which may be hundreds or thousands of dollars lower than what will be paid at the next sale. Thus the catalogs are only guides to prices.

Perhaps the best information concerning the price for stamps comes from the advertisements in publications such as the weekly *Linn's Stamp News* or *Stamps* magazine. The average dealer charge for stamps is more obvious this way. Naturally, unusually high prices for stamps compared with those quoted by others are to be avoided. An unusually low charge for a stamp may reflect poor quality, no matter what the dealer's description. Your best protection comes from being aware of competing prices and buying stamps in the best possible condition for the money.

Inexpensive stamps are best purchased in packets with related material you desire. The cost of packaging and storing single stamps is high. It can greatly increase the price a dealer must charge for a common issue. The price becomes proportionately less in a packet.

TRADE-INS

When you begin buying stamps worth at least several dollars each, you will find that both dealers and collectors may be willing to trade with you while you upgrade your stamp. For example, suppose you have the scarce $1 salmon Columbian commemorative (Scott #241) issued by the United States in 1893. The stamp is used, is lacking gum, and was printed slightly off-center. It is costly, but nowhere near the expense of the mint issue.

A dealer accepting trade-ins might be willing to accept the stamp at its full retail value instead of downgrading your payment by the 15 or 20 percent that would be the normal wholesale to retail markup. You buy the same date and design stamp but in a better quality, adding a few dollars to your trade to meet the difference. Over a period of time, you can trade up to quality stamps you could otherwise not afford.

STAMP CONDITIONS

Stamp conditions are usually described in a number of ways. Mint stamps are those which were never used. However, a mint stamp might have been hinged. Thus a stamp which is exactly as it came from the Post Office would be called "Mint NH (Never Hinged) Original Gum (also marked OG)." If the collector who owned the stamp used a hinge for the mounting but otherwise there is no damage, then the stamp would be "Mint LH (Lightly Hinged) Original Gum." The term "HR" means that there are "Hinge Remnants." The term "Perf OG" usually is used to indicate that only a portion of the original gum has been left on the stamp.

There are other terms as well. Stamps may be categorized as "Extremely Fine," "Very Fine," "Fine," "Very Good," and "Good." What this means varies with the dealers. Stamp grading, theoretically, should be a serious, scientific endeavor that set criteria after almost a century and a half of collecting. However, the reality is that it is a highly subjective field at the moment. Fortunately most dealers follow similar standards and it is possible to approximate an accurate understanding of condition with little training.

Check for the quality of the printing; the margins or white space around the design area; the evenness of the adhesive on the back; creases, tears, or thin areas in the paper; and how the perforations are found. Some stamps are printed in such a way that the perforations actually touch the edge of the design. Other stamps have the design off in a corner with uneven borders. A perfectly centered stamp with even borders, full gum, no creases, no thin areas or other flaws that can occur with the printing process, will be called an Extremely Fine stamp. On the other hand, an occasional crease, uneven margins, poor-quality printing, and perforations cutting into the design will result in a stamp being called Good. Both stamps might be "mint" and "never hinged," but the price a collector will pay for each will vary widely.

Coloring is another factor in condition. Some stamps were printed with inks that fade with time, exposure to light and/or exposure to water. The degree of fading can alter the price a collector is willing to pay and the desirability of the stamp. This is especially true with those stamps extant in large quantity. A rarity will always be desired because the demand is greater than there are stamps available. A common issue that is still available with full original coloring will not be wanted.

WATERMARKS

The watermark is one of the very few technical concerns a beginner need understand. Basically, a watermark is a pattern impregnated in the paper used for making the stamps before the design is printed. In the glossary, laid and wove papers will be explained. Both types can be watermarked.

The main reason for adding watermarks was to help detect counterfeits. Postage stamps have always retained their values in countries regardless of how people have rated their money. When paper money or even coins were being devalued during extreme depressions, stamps have been considered negotiable at their face value. Thus they are a highly desirable item to counterfeit, and governments have tried different methods to make this more difficult. A watermark impregnated in the paper and observable under certain specific conditions is one more tool to prevent dishonesty.

The British have watermarked their paper for almost all their stamps, usually using a simple crown device. The United States felt that such a defense was unnecessary until 1895, when watermarking went into use. Then this method of attempting to foil counterfeiters was stopped in 1918.

Canada, aware of both the United States and Great Britain's efforts with watermarks, felt it unnecessary. Only occasionally have Canadian stamps been watermarked.

Why should you care about watermarks? Two reasons. The first is that it is a counterfeit detector. The second is because some stamps have been printed with two different watermarks. The design is the same, but subsequent printings had two varieties of paper detectable only by looking for the different watermarks. The value difference of the stamps can be astronomical.

There are also some interesting variations in watermarks. Sometimes paper is repaired with tiny threads. This results in a fiber pattern known as a stitch watermark. It is the result of repair, not a deliberate effort to thwart the dishonest.

A second watermark variety occurs when the paper manufacturer, not the Post Office printer, adds a mark to the paper. This is simply the way the manufacturer advertises his paper products.

It is revealed the same way as any other watermark but does not reflect the printing process.

There are two ways to detect most watermarks: Lightly grasp the stamp with your tongs. Then place it face down on a black surface, such as a smooth black tray sold for this purpose. When you do this, you will spot a dark area—the watermark.

The next approach is basically the same as the first. Use the black tray but place a few drops of watermark detector on the stamp to reveal the watermark. Benzine (not benzene) is normally used for this purpose, though benzine will cause the same inks to run that would be affected by soaking with water. Many stamp catalogs and guidebooks state which stamps have such problem inks. If in doubt, or if you can not find the information and the stamps would be expensive to replace, use the special watermark detector fluid available specifically for this purpose.

CAUTION: BENZINE IS EXPLOSIVE! Never use it near cigarettes, candles, or other flames. Use it out-of-doors and store it carefully.

More sophisticated watermark detectors also exist. These use a light source and colored filters. Eventually you may want to invest in such a device if you either decide to buy more expensive stamps or stamps for which watermark variations are the only differences among similar-appearing printings.

PERFORATIONS

There are differences in perforations just as there are differences in watermarks. The spacing of perforations will vary, occasionally, with the same design. Special gauges are sold so that you can measure this; they are inexpensive and as simple to use as a ruler. The gauge comprises many rows of black dots, each row corresponding to a different perforation measurement, and you place the stamp until the perforations exactly match a row of dots.

Since one design may have different perforations and some albums call for both types of stamps, purchase the perforation gauge when you buy your tongs. Fortunately, some dealers provide a gauge at no charge. Also, some albums have a scale printed on one of the pages so you can place the stamp against it to determine the number of perforations along the side.

FAULTS

What can go wrong with a postage stamp? Just about everything. It can tear. Paper gets brittle with age and an old postage stamp may have cuts, scratches on the surface, discoloration, creases, uneven gum, and numerous other problems. A stamp can have a "thin," an area of paper scraped away so that one section of the stamp is thinner than another section.

When you use the watermark tray, most problem areas become evident as well. The stamp held against a dark surface reveals many difficulties. The use of watermark fluid also helps because a thin will appear to be a dark spot separate from the watermark. A crease looks like a line and a tear will be similar in appearance to a crease, though darker.

Repairs of stamps are fairly easy to make by an expert. Paper and glue are layered onto the stamp to rebuild the damaged or thinned area. The details are not important because this takes great skill. It is also an area where fraud is common: a dealer or collector repairing a stamp, then attempting to sell it as flawless.

Some collectors find that a creased stamp can be carefully moistened, then ironed. One mistake and the stamp may be scorched, burned, or otherwise destroyed. However, even when you are successful making the repair, the resale value is greatly reduced. In fact, some rarities command a higher price damaged than they do when the same damage has been repaired.

REGUMMING

So long as there is a demand for a product, people are going to come along to answer that demand. They will sell you the product, even if they have to make it themselves. Such is the case with postage stamps which are in mint condition with full original gum. If some people can not find enough to meet demands, especially early issues, they will be happy to make it for you.

In the early days of philately, collectors were more mature than they are today. They liked stamps because of their design and interesting cancellation, if any. They seldom bothered about the reverse. After all, the reverse was where you applied the gum or glue (early stamps in some instances, never had gum), licked them, and put them on the letter. They were of almost no interest unless someone had torn or otherwise damaged the stamp.

The collectors used hinges to mount their stamps in albums. Other collectors bought both mint and used stamps, knowing that they had been hinged. Everyone did it, the values never changed, and no one cared.

Time passed. There was a new century, stamps had been collected for almost fifty years, and enough collectors had developed to warrant manufacturers trying to find new products to serve them. Along about 1920, one of these products proved to be a new type of mount—a hingeless mount. Stamps could be stored or mounted in albums without disturbing the gum.

A few collectors—a very few collectors—decided that a hingeless mount was essential: it preserved the stamps "Post Office fresh." But it was no big deal and the philatelists were not fanatical about it. They bought hinged stamps because almost all available stamps were hinged. However, they used hingeless mounts for their current acquisitions, their high values, and others. They either kept gummed stamps in perfect condition or they kept previously hinged stamps from being hinged again.

The manufacturers of the new hingeless mounts noticed what was happening and the relatively slow acceptance of their concept. They decided to promote this less-than-essential product by stressing the perfection of stamps (translate that to mean "perfect gum") as the most desirable way to collect. Through the pressure of skilled advertising, more and more collectors were converted to individuals concerned with the backs as well as the designs of the stamps. As a result, the modern collector is "gum happy" at times, and this has led to an interesting problem.

An occasional unscrupulous dealer or collector, skilled in chemistry and out to make a fast dollar, will regum stamps so that they appear never to have been hinged. At first this was relatively easy to detect. Stamps were gummed, then perforated. No adhesive ever seeped over the edges of the paper because there were no holes before the gum had dried.

The people who regummed stamps did not have this luxury. If they brushed the new adhesive to the edge of the paper, tiny amounts would end up spilling over the edge, onto the sides of the perforation marks. This could be detected either with the naked eye or with a magnifying glass.

Experts learned to detect regummed stamps by close observation. This foiled the less skilled among the regummers, who, by the way, continue to apply their "art." The truly skilled regummers took this detection as a challenge. They have now developed ways to regum the stamps so that even a magnifying glass will be of little help. In fact, they have become so skilled that there is a good chance they will fool even the most knowledgeable experts using only ordinary methods for studying them.

The solution to this problem is simple: *Assume that all early-issue stamps, at least those printed before 1920, have been hinged, even if they are otherwise "Mint" or "Mint, Never Hinged."* Assume all such stamps have been regummed. Do not pay a premium for lightly hinged stamps of the same quality or else don't buy stamps in this supposedly "original" condition. A genuinely never-hinged stamp may escape you, but the slim chance is not worth the gamble.

Also check early issues in the Scott or other catalogs to make certain that the gummed (lightly hinged or not) stamp was gummed originally. Many early stamps had no adhesive backing. Some collectors make the assumption that all stamps "had" to be gummed, so the dishonest ones will add gum to all their stamps without it. Knowing that an issue was designed to have no gum when printed will enable you to avoid a problem if the stamp you go to buy has traces of adhesive on a mint condition issue.

Dealers watch for this problem, too. The majority of dealers are honest and knowledgeable. They will usually not purchase such items. If they have them in stock, they will alert you to the addition of the gum if they are aware that this has occurred. Unfortunately, so many thousands of stamps have been issued over the years that an honest dealer might still overlook a stamp where adhesive was added to an issue which was never originally gummed. Thus you must be able to cross-check even the best of dealers when necessary.

ORGANIZATIONS AND SERVICES

Among the checks which can be made concerning stamps are the uses of dealers belonging to organizations which police their own ranks and independent expertising associations. The **American Stamp Dealers' Association** (the ASDA logo is included on members' advertising) is located at 840 Willis Avenue, Albertson, New York 11507.

The expertizing services include:

Friedl Expert Committee, 10 East 40th Street, New York, New York 10016 (worldwide with emphasis on classics).

Society of Philatelic Americans Expertizing Committee, c/o Gordon Torrey, 5118 Duvall Drive, Washington, D.C. 20016 (worldwide).

American Philatelic Expertizing Service, Box 8000, State College, Pennsylvania 16801.

Philatelic Foundation, 270 Madison Avenue, New York, New York 10016.

4

How to Organize, Mount, and Store Your Stamps

The first time you visit a stamp dealer, you will probably want to buy every stamp in sight. The thousands of different stamps will overwhelm you with their color, their beauty, and their historic importance. Some will appeal to you because of their country or origin. Others will feature a topic you enjoy. Whatever the circumstances, you will probably have a difficult time deciding what to save. If you are at all like me, you will simply begin saving everything you find.

Unfortunately, attempting to save everything you encounter creates a problem. You will have tiny pieces of paper everywhere, getting trampled, sucked into the vacuum, eaten by your dog, and subject to numerous other fates. You need a way to organize them.

STAMP HOLDERS

Many collectors start by sorting their stamps according to country, topic, period of history, or whatever other system they devise. They place them in what are known as glassine envelopes, specially made for stamp collectors, or in regular envelopes such as you would send through the mail. The outside of each envelope is labeled and then they are stored inside a shoebox or cigarbox. This is a beginning, but it is not a very effective long-range solution.

The first thing you need to do is to buy an album. Many collectors, myself included, originally licked the backs of mint stamps (stamps in the same condition as when they were purchased from the Post Office) and pasted them in the album. Others tried to use Scotch tape to hold them neatly in place. Unfortunately, both methods ruin the stamps and make them almost impossible to trade or sell.

The answer is to purchase the album that is best suited for your interest. There are several types available, as discussed briefly in the first chapter: these are world, country, topical, and stock albums.

World albums are either very small or run to several volumes. They provide the opportunity for you to collect a representative sampling of the issues of many countries. If you have the interest and the budget, you can even attempt to collect stamps from the earliest British issues through the present, striving for completeness.

Country albums have space for every stamp ever issued by a *single* country. These can be filled more easily and are less discouraging than trying to work with a world album, although the country album is more specialized.

Topical albums allow you to collect stamps related to a specific subject. Such specialized albums are often added as you become more involved with collecting. You may find a specific subject—such as achievements in medicine or outer space—that has special personal appeal. The next logical step is to begin a topical collection with stamps from many countries that share this common theme.

Finally, there are the stock albums. These are special album-style holders that usually contain pages with rows of pockets in which you can insert your stamps. They are designed to hold duplicate stamps you might wish to trade or sell, and also stamps you want to keep but currently have no album to put them in. This can happen if you have only collected United States stamps thus far, for example, and now decide to begin collecting stamps from Great Britain. You only have a United States album and would rather accumulate more British stamps before buying a separate album to hold them. You can store them in the stock book and transfer them when you are ready.

Many companies make albums, including Harris, Scott, Minkus, White Ace, and Lindner. They will differ in design, the thickness of the paper used to make the pages, and the number of illustrations. Some are hingeless—which means they have special holders for each stamp that are made from clear material that provides moisture- and soil-resistant protection for your stamps (usually Mylar is used). The hingeless designs are expensive and unnecessary for a beginner unless you are fortunate enough to have very expensive stamps for which you want to provide the best possible housing.

Hinges provide protection at a lower cost but are time-consuming to use. They are generally preferred when first starting a collection, however.

WHICH ALBUM SHOULD YOU BUY?

The brands and varieties make little difference. Look for the number of stamps illustrated, because the more photographs or drawings in the album, the easier it is to place your stamps. Albums lacking illustrations have a space marked with a number corresponding to that in a catalog, generally Scott. You will have to look up the image of the stamp in the catalog to know which stamp to place in the appropriate space. The illustrated album requires only that you look at the stamp, look at the pictures, then match the stamp to the right image. This saves time and effort. The only problem that you will encounter is when an almost identical stamp is issued several times; then you will have to study the catalog closely.

Your stamp album should be of the loose-leaf variety, either in notebook form or with center posts that are removable to add supplements. This way you can buy new pages each year to keep your collection up-to-date. The center-post albums are better than the notebook variety because they are less easily damaged when accidentally dropped or used over a long period of time. However, you can always move your pages from one album to another when necessary.

You might want to make your own album, buying blank pages or pages with general headings for topical issues. The notebook type is the least expensive. I advise against making your own album at the start, though, because you may encounter the same problem you would have if you were using a shoebox: you may keep changing your mind as to how you want to arrange your stamps. It is more difficult to rearrange a created album than to switch stamps held in glassine envelopes stored in a shoebox.

When you buy a commercial album, your stamps will always look attractive and be housed in an orderly way.

You will want to retain your glassine envelopes or similar holders even after you have an album. Most beginners are on a budget. If you fall into this category, you will want to own a single album to start, protecting your extra stamps as inexpensively as possible. Your old holders will probably prove adequate for now.

Beginners on a budget usually combine one or more general albums with glassine envelopes. These philatelic envelopes are specially designed for holding stamps safely. You can write on the envelopes, they are clear enough to see inside, and they can be filed either in a shoe-box, an index card box, or any other way you choose. They are less expensive than a stock book and serve the same purpose.

HOW TO MOUNT YOUR STAMPS

Rare postage stamps have sold for sums so high that only the very rich can afford them. Stamps in general are considered excellent long-term investments. However, they are also nothing but tiny bits of paper; they are fragile, affected by everything from moisture in the air to the salts and acids of your body, and must be treated with respect in order to maintain their value. This is not a difficult task, but certain procedures must be followed.

First, never touch your postage stamps with your fingers. Use the tongs, mentioned earlier, because the flat, smooth gripping surface causes no harm and is simple to use.

Next, never put anything on a stamp that is not expressly meant for stamp mounting. *Use only peelable hinges made expressly for stamp mounting.* Many a beginner has tried cellophane tape (such as Scotch brand), glue, rubber cement, and numerous other sticking devices. They all either permanently mount the stamp, discolor it, cause it to tear, or otherwise destroy its value as a collectible. Hinges cost a tiny fraction of a cent each and are well worth the money. Later, when you have some special stamps you want to protect without using a hinge, you can buy the more expensive crystal-clear mounts mentioned previously.

Using a hinge is easy. Buy the prefolded variety, which has a short end to be moistened lightly and attached to the stamp, as well as a longer side, which is moistened and used to attach the stamp to the album page. If you have a regular hinge, you can use your tongs to fold a ¼-inch flap, which you attach to the stamp. You use the longer side to mount the stamp in the album. Most philatelists do not moisten the entire long portion of the regular or prefolded hinge, even though it is gummed to allow for such an action. Moistening just a small portion makes it easier to peel the hinge from the album.

A peelable hinge leaves no paper traces on the stamp. This is important because you want the stamp damaged as little as possible. A mint stamp or even a canceled stamp retaining vestiges of its original gum will have that gum disturbed by any hinge. When the hinge is not readily removable, the damage is somewhat greater than it needs to be.

Some stamps are triangular. Mounting these is more difficult because of the odd format. However, it is really just a matter of angling the hinge. Mount the hinge so that the fold of the hinge is aimed toward the center of the album. This means that if a triangular stamp is mounted on a left album page, the hinge fold should be at the right side of the triangle so it is aimed toward the center when mounted. A triangular stamp on the right side of the album will have the hinge on the left of the stamp, the fold toward the center. The reason for this is not some mystical rite of philately. It simply ensures that when the album is closed, the stamp will lie flat, with limited risk of being bent.

Blocks of stamps or strips of stamps will need more than one hinge. Often a block is mounted with one hinge at the top and one at the bottom so that it does not move in the album. This prevents the reverse from being studied without removing the stamp from the album. However, the only time anyone will want to see the reverse is when a stamp is being sold, so this is no problem. You can also use two or more hinges across the top or whatever other arrangements seem best for the stamps being mounted. *Always use as few hinges as possible.*

The same situation exists with covers and souvenir sheets or cards. Most souvenir sheets are small enough so that hinges can be used. If the souvenir sheet seems likely to rise in value, try using a hingeless mount into which the sheet is inserted.

Use with caution all hingeless mounts requiring the stamp or souvenir sheet to be inserted in a special sleeve (often made from chemically inert mylar). The reason is that it is easy to bend the

It is doubtful that you will want to remove a souvenir sheet from its covers in order to mount them, used, in your album. Should this kind of situation occur, treat the covers as you would the stamps.

corners of the stamp or sheet when inserting it into the sleeve. It is also easy to wrinkle the stamp or add an unwanted fold.

Make certain that you use the correct-size mount, not one that is so tight that the stamp buckles. Slightly loose is better than too snug. Never seal the ends with cellophane tape, paper clips, or staples. Such items and others like them will in time likely damage your stamps.

REMOVING PAPER

Earlier I mentioned stamps being "off paper." Used stamps will have been attached to an envelope or mailing wrapper of some sort. Collectors want to remove this paper before mounting their stamps. It looks better, avoids the problem of trying to cut the paper so it is trimmed to match the stamp size, prevents perforations from being damaged, and makes for a less bulky album.

There are a number of ways to remove paper from stamps. The biggest problem is trying to avoid the pitfalls of both tears and running inks. Just peeling a stamp from paper is likely to tear the stamp. Soaking the stamp in water is fine if the inks are stable, but many inks will run. This is because, among other problems, the use of aniline ink results in runs, as will occur with stamps printed on chalky paper (many British colonial stamps and Russian stamps from 1858 to 1875 have this problem, for instance). Britain used fugitive inks in 1883, 1884, and 1900, a fact repeated by other countries such as the Dutch Indies (in the Queen Wilhelmina stamp designs of 1933–1937, e.g.). Many photogravure stamps, watercolor prints, and stamps on safety paper will run. Sometimes the problem is only with a portion of a series, such as the 30-cent, $1.00, and $4.00 Columbian issues produced by the United States in 1893 as part of a larger series of Columbian Exposition commemoratives. But just because some stamps in a series are safe to soak does not mean they all are.

All you need to safely soak stamps is a shallow tray of the type used by photographers for developing prints. These are quite reasonably priced in photography stores. *Use the tray for your collection only,* even if you or a member of your family has photography as a hobby. The chemistry for photography can damage the stamps even after cleaning and drying the tray.

Do not fully immerse stamps in water, because they may run.

Instead, place them on the water so that the paper becomes moist, not the stamp. Use cool or warm water to further soften the gum, but never use hot water.

There are three good ways to proceed once the paper is moist enough for removal. Use the first two for large quantities of stamps and the third for certain special stamps. Practice with inexpensive stamps until you see which is easier for you. Extremely rare stamps are seldom found on paper.

Soak the stamp, assuming that the ink or cancelation will not run: then peel the paper from the stamp. ALWAYS PEEL PAPER FROM STAMPS, NOT STAMPS FROM PAPER. THIS PREVENTS TEARING.

Lay the stamp on a clean piece of blotting paper, face-down. Bend a small edge of the *paper, not the stamp,* with your stamp tongs. The gum should be soft enough after a few minutes of soaking to allow you to peel the paper. If it is not yet soft, do not force it. Instead, resoak the stamp until the paper is removable.

Once the paper is peeled, dry the stamp between the pages of clean blotting paper, such as is available from camera stores. Do not use advertising blotters: they are of poor quality, seldom are adequately absorbent, and often have inks used for the message which can discolor the stamps.

Use two trays, each partially filled with water. Soak a color-fast stamp in the one (several may be soaked at once with either method, as long as you are careful to not let them bunch together). Then use an artist's brush to gently submerge the stamp, face-down, against the bottom of the tray. Gently rub the brush against the back to remove loose paper. Much of all of the paper will be removed at this time.

Use your tongs to transfer the stamp to the other tray, again floating it with the paper-side down. After a few minutes, use the brush to place it at the bottom, face-down, while you gently remove the rest of the paper.

Finally, transfer the stamp to your blotter book. After a few minutes between the pages, you should be able to remove the clean, dry, flat stamp with your tongs. If some gum remains, you may have to gently work it off with a little effort. Be careful to not damage the stamp.

Sound a little difficult, especially with the warnings about not damaging the stamps? It is. That is why most collectors buy stamps off-paper and avoid the potential problems.

Use a humidor box for stamps that are likely to have non-fast inks and other problems. It is sold by many stamp dealers and has an absorbent paper bottom (some of the boxes require you to line the bottom yourself, using sheets of blotting paper you will dampen yourself). Fit the stamp on a grated shelf or directly on the extremely moist blotting paper, depending upon the type of box you buy. In either case, the stamp is always face-up, so the paper to be removed is exposed to the moisture. After several minutes, it will be easy to remove the paper from the stamps and place the stamps on your blotters.

Some stamps have minor creases and folds. Do not buy such stamps if they would normally have high value, because such a problem is always detectable, even after you correct it. However, you may want to repair other stamps. Moisten the area with the fold. When the paper is soft, gently flattening the fold with a brush, tongs, or an iron. (Be careful not to burn the stamp!)

Some early stamps have inks that will discolor to a brown or black from their original yellow, red, orange, or, occasionally, blue. Atmospheric sulfur is the usual cause of this condition, which may be reversible.

The answer to the sulfur problem may be the 2 percent hydrogen peroxide solution available at little cost from your local pharmacy. Use a small artist's brush, dip it in the peroxide, remove the excess liquid from the bristles, then *lightly* "paint" the stamp. Do not get any remaining gum wet.

Leave the thin coating of peroxide on the stamp for a minute or two; then clean your brush in fresh water and use the wet brush to apply clean water to the surface of the stamp. This should be an *extremely thin* coating, just to make sure the action of the peroxide has ceased. Use a blotter to dry the stamp and keep it from curling.

HOW TO STORE YOUR STAMPS

Postage stamps should be stored with care. You must consider both theft and damage from improper handling, though improper handling is usually the greater risk. The wrong storage conditions can cause stamps to stick to one another, become creased and/or torn.

It is best to limit the pressure on your stamps when the album is closed. This means not filling your album with more pages than it can realistically hold. Center-post albums generally hold more pages than notebook-style albums. It is always cheaper to buy extra binders than to have to replace damaged stamps.

Store your albums in an upright position when possible. If they are placed on their side, do not pile other albums, books, or anything else on top of them. The extra weight will cause damage.

Select a room which has a moderate temperature all-year-round. Any area that averages approximately 70 to 75 degrees and has a low humidity will be good for storage. A home that is air-conditioned in the potentially humid summer months should have the album in any room where the air-conditioning is regularly working. Should you live in a dry climate, there are what is known as swamp coolers that reduce the room temperature by having a fan blow air across a moist pad. This raises the moisture level of the air and you should make certain such a device is not damaging your stamps. If need be, leave a few inexpensive, replaceable mint stamps in such a room to see if there are any problems. Whenever the outside humidity is high, only refrigerated air-conditioning should be used around the stamps. Usually the increase in moisture created by combining a swamp cooler with a dry climate is not very damaging.

Keep loose stamps out of the bright sunlight. If you have a wall display with stamps, hang it so the direct sun will not strike it since this light can damage the colors over time.

Keep valuable stamps in a bank safety-deposit box, either on an album page or in a glassine envelope or similar holder. Some collectors like to make a Xerox copy of the page on which their valuable stamps are kept, placing the page with the stamp in the safety-deposit box and the Xerox copy in their albums. Keeping valuable stamps safely put away in this manner reduces the chance of theft or loss by fire.

When you acquire valuable stamps, you may want to specially insure your collection. Most insurance companies handling hobby portions of homeowner's and renter's policies are limited in the coverage they will provide. They are also fairly expensive if your collection is large.

Collectors needing insurance are well advised to join the American Philatelic Society, P.O. Box 800, State College, Pennsylvania 16801. The group insurance plan for stamp collectors is so reasonable that even when the cost of membership is added, you come out ahead. The insurance will also vary with your storage, though, and keeping valuable stamps at home will make you a higher risk. One alternative to the safety-deposit box is to have a good home safe with fire protection in order to reduce your cost to some degree. However, the savings and security are greatest when you insure stamps, the rarities of which are kept in the safety-deposit box in your bank. The other precautions necessary for storing your stamps are all common sense. Keep them away from small children who may lick the adhesive or glue them to the walls. Likewise, it is best to avoid using them near a pet. My miniature Schnauzer ate twelve stamps and part of an album cover before I realized that perhaps a higher shelf would be more realistic for storage.

Extra stamps are best stored in glassine envelopes and placed in any holder that keeps them from being damaged. This can range from a shoebox to a file box normally meant for 3x5 index cards. As long as the glassine holders will not be jammed together, you should have no problems.

Some collectors like to begin with envelopes as holders. They take old ones, remove the stamp, and then use the envelopes as they would glassines. This is fine for common stamps, although the adhesive and acid content of normal envelope paper could be a danger when attempting to store more valuable issues.

5

U.S. Stamps

The first postage stamps for the United States were issued in 1847 and honored Benjamin Franklin. The reason was that Franklin was the first major force in attempting to use the mails to link the various colonies and settlements which eventually united in rebellion against the British. He created 24-hour-a-day postal service to improve the movement of the mail, the use of special boats to link mail service between the Continental Congress in Philadelphia and the Southern colonies, and managed to generate a profit while providing better service. It was a natural idea to honor him on the next major innovation in American mail—the prepaid postage stamp.

THE EARLIEST STAMPS

The value of the prepaid stamp moving mail by the ounce, regardless of distance within certain mileage zones, can be fully understood by reading Chapter 12, which discusses how messages had been sent in the past. These new stamps represented a radical improvement. A 5-cent postage stamp would handle a first-class letter for up to 300 miles. Ten cents in postage would be used for sending letters to any distance greater than that.

The first stamp, a 5-cent imperforate with Benjamin Franklin's portrait, is found with various other shadings resulting from the printing process. The stamps were used in such quantity that they are not rarities, but a high-quality specimen of a canceled 5-cent Franklin stamp will still cost you a sum in the range of four figures.

It is believed that the printing plate used to make the 5-cent was damaged by the ink. All the impressions are of poor quality, although a 10-cent stamp issued that same year is generally excellent, whether new or used.

Most of the early cancellations were done with pen and ink, often rather lightly, and there are many examples of canceled stamps having the ink "erased" to increase their selling price. The "erasing" or cleaning of such stamps is a complex procedure not usually obvious to the untrained observer, so an expert's evaluation should be obtained before purchasing such items.

The early changes in United States postage stamps often represented a reduction in the cost of mailing. The first change came in 1851 when the 5-cent rate was applied to mail traveling by ship, surface mailing being reduced to a 3-cent charge. A 1-cent rate was used for mail going from post office to post office instead of home delivery and the 10-cent stamp remained for coast-to-coast mailing. A 12-cent stamp was added for foreign mailing. As with the earlier issues, all these were imperforate, that is straight-edged on all sides.

Most of these early stamps have numerous varieties. The 1851 1-cent blue Franklin stamp has so many die and plate printing varieties (there are eight major types) that you can get what appears at first glance to be the same stamp and have it worth either five figures or perhaps only $50, depending upon which type it is. Entire books are available showing the plate differences, cancellation mark changes, and other factors. However, most beginners have little interest in such matters other than to be aware that they exist. A catalog, such as the annual *Scott U.S. Specialized Catalog,* will have detailed illustrations showing the major design differences for those early issues. You should study

Benjamin Franklin has been honored with numerous commemorative stamps, including this 1851 issue, which is now a great rarity.

these closely in order to gain an understanding of the development of early United States stamps.

Perforations of some American stamps began in 1857. There have been attempts at fraud, eliminating the perforations in order to give the impression that the Franklin head stamp known as Scott #18 was actually the rare #5 imperforate. This problem became so severe that later the design of the #18 was slightly modified to make any alteration easier to identify. Actually a serious study of each of these designs will show radical differences, such as the characteristic doubling of the design of the #5 because of problems with the die on the plate. However, you should remain aware of the alterations.

The early high-value stamps of 1857—the 24-cent (Scott #37), 30-cent (Scott #38), and 90-cent (Scott #39) denominations—are extremely scarce. Demand was never very great during this period and a number of these stamps were destroyed. The 90-cent deep-blue Washington head stamp, for example, started with just 29,000 printed.

One of the problems with the 1857 stamps was that they were demonetized to prevent the Confederates from using them, causing many people to destroy them. During the first months of 1861, as the North and South prepared for war, Southern United States Post Offices were closed by the Union. Confederate Postmaster General John Reagan wanted to make an orderly transition to maintain good relations for the day—which he perceived to be coming—when there would be two separate countries comprising what had been the United States. Union stamps were to be returned and eventually there would be mail service with both Confederate States stamps and Union postage, everyone operating much the same as with mail that traveled from the U.S. to Europe. History now shows the idea was unworkable.

THE PONY EXPRESS

Before discussing the Civil War, it is important to mention one of the most colorful of the short-term activities of the U.S. Postal Service. This was the idea of the Pony Express.

The Pony Express was introduced at a time when the nation was becoming both physically and emotionally divided. The emotional division was caused by the impending Civil War between the Northern free states and the Southern slave-holding states. The physical division was caused by gold and silver discoveries on the West Coast. Migration to San Francisco and other boom towns was so great that people were becoming separated from their loved ones. Personal communication and business correspondence took a long period of time, sometimes over three weeks on long routes in bad weather. There were also problems with Indian attacks, hostile weather and difficult terrain. The Overland Telegraph was being constructed, an operation which meant that news could eventually be relayed from coast to coast much easier than in the past. But right now, the idea that a horse and rider could accomplish something that had failed all others was intriguing to the public. It was a daring adventure which, if it worked, would change the preconceived notions of hundreds of thousands of individuals.

The idea behind the Pony Express was genius in its simplicity. No expense would be spared in obtaining men and horses capable of the ultimate endurance under stress. The animals—some ponies, others not—were chosen for speed, health, stamina, and other factors that would allow them to be run at top speed between relay stations set approximately fifteen miles apart. The service was launched April 3, 1860, with a run from St. Joseph, Missouri, to Sacramento, California.

One of the most famous riders was William F. Cody, later to gain international fame as Buffalo Bill, who showed true heroism as a genuine Pony Express rider.

Cody first served as a substitute rider when the Pony Express began. Later he went to Laramie, Wyoming, where he was hired full-time to handle the 76-mile run between Red Buttes and Three Crossings. This was a potentially dangerous area, but Cody rode without mishap for several weeks. Then, many round trips after starting, he reached the Three Crossings Terminal and discovered that the courier who was to continue the ride had been killed. Cody mounted a fresh horse and began the run that would take him 86 miles to Rocky Ridge. Each rider had a set distance to cover, only stopping long enough to change mounts at the specified intervals. This meant a ride of 162 miles without stopping.

Cody reached his destination, then returned along the full dual route. He completed 322 miles without meaningful rest, the longest ride known to have been completed by a single rider.

Most of the mail carried by the Pony Express riders was so

costly to send that it involved extremely thin paper, not special packages. Charges of $5 per half ounce of mail were common at the start. However, such was the myth of the Pony Express that the public believed the horses might be carrying almost anything of value, including large sums of money. The riders, including Cody, knew that when such rumors were in the air, bandits would probably strike.

Cody was concerned about a possible problem so he decided to protect the mail by carrying a second mochila (a leather container with locking pockets). The first, containing the mail, was hidden under his saddle. The second, carried in the normal way, was stuffed with paper.

The fear of road agents was well founded. Cody was stopped at gunpoint and ordered to turn over the mochila. Cody tried to talk them out of the robbery, stressing the sanctity of the U.S. mail and the terrible situation they were creating with the robbery. The men would hear none of such talk from a mere boy and insisted the mochila be turned over so they would not have to kill the youth.

Finally Cody gave in. He tossed the mochila, then shot one of the men. He kicked his horse and rode over the robber who was on the ground, taking the pouch. He was out of range before they could shoot at him, the real mail pouch still hidden when he arrived at the next station, ahead of schedule.

By October of 1861, the Pony Express was no longer viable. The telegraph spanned the nation and, with the setting of the last pole, communication from coast to coast was possible. A mail service was still necessary but the public and the government knew that trains and stagecoaches could handle nonessential service. The telegraph would communicate the urgent messages that required immediate transmittal from coast to coast.

For the collector, there is a legacy from the Pony Express. Numerous covers stamped with the Pony Express symbol (a racing horse and rider), the date, and origin of the trip exist. Many show the various links with the various stage companies as well, such as the Central Overland California and Pike's Peak Express Company or the Butterfield Overland Mail. All add a rich legacy both for enjoyment and for collecting by those interested in this unique period of American postal history.

The most interesting modern cover related to the Pony Express might be the one designed in 1940 for the release of the postage stamp listed in the Scott Catalog as #894. This 3-cent henna brown stamp was meant to commemorate the 80th Anniversary of the Pony Express. It was released on the First Day of Issue in both St. Joseph, Missouri, and Sacramento, California. These were the connecting points for the riders who were expected to make the journey in 10 days. Many of the envelopes bear a cachet showing a map of the territory involved and are postmarked with one or the other cities.

The Overland Mail was celebrated on a 4-cent crimson rose postage stamp issued in 1958 (Scott #1120), the 100th Anniversary of the route. A team of horses pulling the mail coach while the guards fight off unknown attackers is shown.

Many collectors are familiar with the 1869 stamp (Scott 113) featuring a mail carrier on horseback. This 2-cent regular issue, the first with a design other than a portrait, is often believed to be a Pony Express rider. However, the drawing is simply that of a standard post rider and horse traveling with a load of letters.

CIVIL WAR POSTAGE

The short-lived Pony Express was the most interesting mail carrier, but the Civil War produced some unusual circumstances for the mail. These have resulted in a wide variety of postal issues, special stamps, and odd uses for stamps in the economy.

First came the problem of Southern postmasters refusing to worry about returning stamps on hand to the North where, technically, they belonged. The Northern postal officials did not expect compliance with the return order. They arranged for the issuance of new stamps, the old to be exchanged at face value for a set period of time. After that, all the former stamps were to be demonetized. This means that, technically, only stamps printed from 1861 to date are legal for use on letters.

The problems the Post Office faced during the Civil War have left a wealth of collectibles for us to enjoy. Stamps were used as money, including for pocket change. There were patriotic envelopes with cartoons and other forms of satiric art. There were special provisionals made by the postmasters and numerous other items. Many of these are still extremely inexpensive and it is possible for a beginner to put together a nice display of these various items.

Many of the Southern postmasters developed a system for proving that postage had been paid even though there were no stamps. They would sometimes make a mark on the envelope or they would cut their own crude stamps from pieces of wood or similar materials. Even change had to be handmade because coins were hoarded. In one case, that of New Orleans, Louisiana, Postmaster John Riddell, special paper money was created for change. He had 15 denominations of notes made up, their values ranging from 1 cent to 5 dollars. These included both a 48-cent note and a 50-cent note, all signed by Postal Clerk Ed Rapier. They bore the statement: "Receivable in payment of postage, and redeemable at the New Orleans Post Office."

Riddell also had postage stamps printed by John Childs, a New Orleans printer and engraver. The 5-cent stamps were printed on sheets of 40. The 5-cent denomination could be used for sending letters less than 500 miles. Ten cents' postage had to be used for distances in excess of 500 miles.

Riddell also had 2-cent stamps printed, though these were not released right away. It was so unusual to have privately printed stamps used at the Post Office that Riddell was uncertain how the public would react. When his idea proved successful, Riddell formally requested permission to officially print Confederate-approved stamps for his use.

These stamps, available to collectors of Civil War postal issues, were an immediate success. They cost $41 and generated sales in excess of $500 the first day. However, they were considered worthless by critics of the New Orleans concept in other cities within Louisiana. Riddell defended himself, saying:

"The stamps issued are intended only for drop letters in the New Orleans Post Office and to facilitate operations at the office. For local purposes they are not 'perfectly worthless.' For others, they are not designed, and it is not pretended that they will pay for any letter dropped at another office."

Eventually Riddell had to add the inscription "USABLE EXCLUSIVELY IN THE NEW ORLEANS POST OFFICE" to the margins of each sheet of stamps. This was of little value, though, because once the stamps were cut from the sheets, the marginal inscriptions were meaningless.

The New Orleans effort was short-lived because Riddell was active only a year. However, other experiments were taking place.

STAMPS AS MONEY

In the North, writer Horace Greeley suggested that postage stamps be used as small change. His column, appearing in the *New York Tribune*, talked of placing postage stamps pasted onto "light vellum paper" into circulation, the stamps, legal government issues of accepted value, could replace them.

On July 17, 1862, Congress passed a law allowing postage stamps to be used as legal tender. However, what was not considered by anyone were the problems. The Post Office did not have adequate stamps for mail. Then the public began using them for change and compounded the difficulties they were facing. Even worse, as stamps became dirty and stuck together, the public expected to be able to turn them in for fresh stamps. This meant trying to sort through blobs of illegible paper in addition to the other problems.

The magnitude of the problem for the Post Office can be seen from just the New York City branch. On a normal day, $3,000 in stamps would be sold to cover business and personal needs within the city. Once the law went into effect, the sales jumped to $24,000 in stamps in a day.

The Post Office fought back, refusing to accept payment in anything other than legal government-issue money, which few people had. The most common currency still in circulation was a $5 bill, forcing $5 to be the minimum purchase.

On August 12, 1862, a man named John Gault thought he had an answer for everyone. He developed a round metal case which could hold a postage stamp. A thin sliver of almost transparent mica served as a cover, the metal holder's edge bent just enough to hold the mica in place. The face value of the stamp would serve as change. The stamp plus holder, in effect, became a coin.

Gault's idea was to have merchants buy his holders, each filled with a stamp of a different denomination to serve the need for change. The merchants would have an advertising message added to the back, which many companies did. They then marked up their merchandise to compensate for the cost of the case and gave the encased postage stamps to customers as change.

These encased postage stamps are still available from stamp and coin dealers, since they are a curious hybrid of both. The selling prices are usually $300 and up, depending on their quality.

The encased postage stamps were immensely popular, much to the disgust of the Postmaster General, Montgomery Blair. He arbitrarily ordered the local post offices to stop selling large quantities of stamps to people such as Gault. He said that they could only sell to previous, regular customers, and even then, they could only sell in quantities roughly equal to the number of stamps purchased before they were used for legal tender.

POSTAL CURRENCY

Eventually the U.S. government compensated by printing what was known as "postage currency." These were special stamps each measuring 2¾ inches by 3⅜ inches, printed on both sides of heavy paper. Several of these stamps were printed to a sheet, with denominations including 5, 10, 25, and 50 cents. They were perforated at first, but later issues were produced without perforations, requiring that they be cut. Many people cut their sheets into blocks worth $1 each for easier handling.

The design of the postage currency, collected today by both stamp collectors interested in the Civil War, and coin collectors interested in fractional currency, matched the designs of the stamps. There were 10-cent stamps bearing the portrait of George Washington in circulation at the time. These portraits were reproduced singly on the 10-cent postage currency and they were repeated five times on the 50-cent postage currency.

The postage currency eventually became standard pocket change. It was accepted at face value because it related to postal issues and the public had faith in stamps. At the same time, it stopped the need for using postage stamps in place of the hoarded small change.

Other forms of Civil War postal collectibles include "prisoner-of-war covers," which are envelopes mailed by prisoners of war; "patriotic covers," which were envelopes bearing a satiric or inspirational slogan or cartoon; and even "flag of truce" mail. These were letters sent from one side to the other by special arrangement and resulted in the envelopes bearing both Northern and Southern stamps. A few flag of truce covers exist with the stamp on one side and a coin equal to the cost of the additional postage required.

Envelopes sent during the Civil War have special appeal. This cover has an 1861 3-cent stamp honoring George Washington. The cancellation is a target design popular with collectors, some of whom pay a premium when the cancellation hits the stamp in the exact center (called a "bullet" cancellation).

While the Civil War brought numerous problems for the Post Office Department and fascinating historical mail items for us, work on standard issues for the mail continued. For example, the first United States stamps of 1861 were essays, examples of what the final printing would be like. The National Bank Note Company was handling the task of designing the new stamps, and the essays, released in August, were on brittle, thin paper. They are in denominations ranging from 1 cent to 90 cents and all are easily damaged. They are considered postal issues and catalogued accordingly, although they were never meant for circulation.

BLACK JACKS

The Southern postmasters were frequently bitter about the start of the Civil War and did not bother accounting for the U.S. stamps on hand. The Northern postal officials did not expect compliance. They arranged for the issue of new stamps, the old to be exchanged at face value for a set period of time. After that, all the former stamps were to be demonetized. As mentioned before, this means that, technically, only stamps printed from 1861 to date are legal for use on letters.

September 1861 saw the release of the regular issues. They were well printed on good-quality paper and remain relatively inexpensive for many issues in used condition. The most famous of the stamps planned during this period is the 2-cent stamp featuring Andrew Jackson, which was not actually released until July 1, 1863. This is nicknamed the "Black Jack" because of the black background.

A "Black Jack"—a 2-cent stamp featuring Andrew Jackson. This stamp makes a good investment.

Most Black Jacks found are poorly centered. There are double transfers and numerous other problems with the vast majority of the 250 million stamps printed. The varieties are so great that there are specialists in this field who have vast collections of different Black Jacks. There are even bisected examples found regularly on envelopes. The 2-cent stamp was cut so that it could be combined with a second stamp and used for 3-cent postage letters. This was a common solution when a 1-cent stamp was not available, and so long as the stamp was cut completely in half, there were no complaints from the Post Office.

The 3-cent rose-colored Washington stamp of 1861, catalogued as #65 in Scott, is probably the most popular of the Civil War era issues. A used copy is readily found for around a dollar, less than the cost of many contemporary stamps. The low cost and historic significance have led collectors to buy these stamps for their cancellation variations, including the different cities where they were used.

There are seemingly endless varieties of the stamps of 1861. These range from those canceled with the word "Hiogo," indicating that they were used for trade in the Japanese Post Office mail, to extremely thin varieties. The latter are not caused by special printings but rather by the forced removal of stamps from envelopes. Collectors often used a sharp blade to remove the stamps, eliminating much of the paper as well.

Fear of counterfeiting led to the introduction of tiny cuts throughout the paper so that each postage stamp would have an area with perhaps 200 or more tiny cuts. This was known as grillwork and it was used in 1867, the designs remaining the same as the ones from 1861. This grillwork is usually seen most easily by lighting the stamp and holding it against a dark background.

PICTORIALS

The 1869 stamps are the first that have a strong appeal to collectors of pictorials. These introduced a radical design concept for the time. The stamps would show scenes from the past to make them visually interesting as well as functional. It was a major cause for the growing interest in stamp collecting in this country.

The stamps showed such scenes as the landing of Columbus, the signing of the Declaration of Independence, a post rider and horse, a locomotive, and the steamship S. S. *Adriatic*, among others. Eleven stamps were introduced in all, their values ranging from 1 cent to 90 cents, only three of the issues (the Franklin 1-cent, Washington 6-cent, and Lincoln 90-cent) having traditional portraits. The rest were scenes, a concept that had not yet been tried elsewhere in the world. These were also the first bicolor U.S. stamps. Unfortunately, this innovation did not last for long and it was 1893 before the next series of pictorials was attempted.

In 1870, stamps were issued in what became popularly known as the "Bank Notes" series. This is because this single series of stamps were printed by three different bank note companies over the twenty-year life of the designs. The basic designs are the same but the printing varies. For example, the National Bank Note

Columbus' discovery of America is honored on these postage stamps issued for the World's Columbian Exposition in 1892.

Company used grilled paper when printing Scott #134–144 but did not use grilled paper for Scott #145-155. Then the stamp printing was switched to the Continental Bank Note Company, which used the same design but added "secret marks" to distinguish their plates from the earlier ones. For example, the 1-cent stamp showing Franklin (Scott #156) has a hidden mark in the pearl to the left of the numeral "1." This is a small crescent which does not exist in the seemingly identical Scott #145. Each hidden identification mark, and one exists for each of the low values, is easily seen by checking catalogs such as Scott, where the marks are illustrated.

The American Bank Note Company chose a different approach when they printed Scott #182-191. A switch to a soft porous yellowish paper quickly shows the difference. A watermark detector is easily used to spot the distinctive weave.

There are numerous printings and many slight variations because of the great number of years that these stamps were utilized. Again this can be an entire collecting specialty because of subtle changes in color, printing plates, and other technical aspects.

You will spot the term "reissues" in your stamp catalog in relation to the early stamps. This relates to a public relations concept the Post Office developed for the 1875 Centennial celebration held in Philadelphia. Stamp collecting had become a small business, but one of which many people were aware. Only a few full-time dealers were operating yet many people enjoyed stamps. The Post Office Department thought that they could reissue all the stamps that had been printed up to that time, so that collectors and souvenir hunters could buy them. It was assumed that few, if any, of these reissues would be used to send letters; therefore there would be great profit, as well as satisfying an interest in the early stamps. Different paper and different colored inks were used to ensure that there was no confusion with the originals. The Post Office did not want to be accused of counterfeiting its own products.

Sales of the reissues and reproductions (technically, a reissue needs original dies, and, in some cases, new dies had to be made) were not particularly successful. They are fairly scarce but, fortunately for collectors, underpriced for their relative rarity. They are not sold with enough frequency to be advertised heavily. Collectors do not hear about them very often, demand is low, keeping the price down.

By 1890, printing techniques changed in the Post Office and the stamps became more consistent throughout the run of a particular design. Collectors today are more likely to concentrate on collecting a wide variety of different issues than endless variations of the same design.

COMMEMORATIVES

The most popular of the early stamps coming from this newly improved mechanical era are the stamps from the Columbian Exposition. The series of sixteen commemoratives shows the history of Columbus' voyage to the New World. The story of the Exposition is covered earlier in this book. The stamps were not popular for the first few years after their sale, despite the fact that printings were not high for the $4 and $5 stamps. Then, as the number of collectors increased, having the first commemorative series became desirable. Prices steadily rose, especially for the higher values, which were found to be generally defective (thins, creases, and other problems).

The Bureau of Printing and Engraving took over the production of stamps in 1894. The first issues, produced from engraving dies supplied by the American Bank Note Company, are popular with collectors. They were poorly made at first and limited in number, the result of the Bureau learning a skill previously handled by outsiders. The better the quality of the issue in terms of centering and similar details, the greater the price.

The remainder of the U.S. issues fall into two categories, the fairly standard stamps issued for regular postage and the commemoratives. Air mail, special delivery, and other specialized categories are either collected as a unique specialty by many (air mail, e.g.) or considered only when completeness of a country's collection is desired.

The commemoratives have the greatest appeal because of the quality and detail of the artwork. For example, the Trans-Mississippi Exposition of 1898—these nine stamps tell the story of life in the western part of the United States, including the $1 stamp, Western cattle in a storm, which is considered one of the most beautiful stamps ever printed. It was designed after the painting *The Vanguard* by J. A. MacWhirter. Others in the series include Indian hunting buffalo, troops guarding a train, the hardships of emigration, Fremont on the Rocky Mountains, Marquette on the Mississippi, Western mining prospector (after the famous Frederic Remington painting *The Gold Bug*), and the Mississippi River Bridge.

Most of the early commemoratives were connected with a specific exposition and each issue had several different stamps relating to the same theme. These include the Pan-American Exposition of 1901, the Louisiana Purchase Exposition of 1904, the Jamestown Exposition of 1907, and others. Gradually, in the late 1920's and early 1930's, the multi-stamp theme approach became less popular and commemoratives were issued for single events. There is the Mothers of America issue featuring the painting of *Whistler's Mother* (Scott #737; Mother's Day, 1934), the Texas Centennial issue showing Sam Houston, Stephen Austin, and the Alamo (Scott #776, 1936), and others. However, groups of stamps for a specific event still continued, interspersed with the singles. These included the National Parks issues (Scott #740–749, 1934), the Army/Navy issues (Scott #785–794, 1937), and others.

One of the most popular series of commemoratives featuring portraits was the Famous Americans issues of 1939–1940. Well-known authors, poets, educators, scientists, composers, artists, and inventors were commemorated. These issues range from Scott #859 (Washington Irving) through #893 (Alexander Graham Bell) before returning to the single, elaborately designed concepts, such as the stamp for Pony Express rider (Scott #894), Pan American Union stamp showing the Three Graces from Botticelli's *Primavera*—"Spring" (Scott #895), and others.

Two years before Davis Scott and James Irwin used the Apollo 15 mission to establish a post office on the moon, Edwin Aldrin, Jr., and Neil Armstrong became the first humans to set foot on the moon. This stamp honors their 1969 feat.

Modern commemoratives are seldom rare. Too many stamps are printed and too many collectors save mint issues for the value to be great. However, interesting deviations from normal issue patterns always have a strong appeal. For example, the 1967 Space Accomplishments issues, which are a se-tenant pair, requiring two stamps to show the full scene of the space-walking astronaut and *Gemini 4* capsule (Scott #1331–1332), have been quite popular as a pair, the value of the se-tenant much higher than for the individual stamps. The lunar landing was also commemorated as a se-tenant with Scott #1434–1435, 1971. The 1976 full sheet of the Bicentennial state flags (Scott #1633–1682) commands a premium over the individual issues, though smaller groups, such as the 1974 block of eight letter-writing stamps after famous paintings in honor of the Centenary of the Universal Postal Union (Scott #1530–1537) or the 1975 block of four stamps showing Continental military uniforms for the Bicentenary of U.S. Military Services (Scott #1565–1568), have not shown a premium in blocks over the single issues.

The inexpensive nature of United States commemoratives and their wide variety are what have given them their appeal. These stamps, along with some of the experimental special-issue varieties, such as the 1976 American Bicentennial Issue Souvenir Sheets (Scott #1686–1689), have made collecting United States stamps a major interest of philatelists throughout the world.

Today American stamps continue to follow popular themes. Efforts are made to appeal to the broadest base of interest, whether it be a design featuring the Touro Synagogue in Newport, Rhode Island, the oldest temple in America, or proposed stamps (at this writing) for band leader Glenn Miller, boxers Joe Louis and Rocky Marciano, and various politicians. The stamp designs are planned through the help of the Citizens' Stamp Advisory Committee, c/o Stamps Division, U.S. Postal Service, Washington, D.C. 20260.

You, as a new collector, can have input into stamp design. You may propose a particular design or subject for a commemorative, sending your idea (a sketch is not necessary) along with the reasons why you feel the design should be considered, to the address given above. If your proposal meets with approval, one day you may see your idea commemorated on a stamp moving the mail across the nation and around the world.

6

British Stamps

Whenever you think of postal history, you must first think of Great Britain. It was there, in the mid-nineteenth century, that the modern concept of a mail system accessible to everyone, at a price realistic for all, was developed.

The British innovations were partially out of necessity. It is difficult to imagine a mail system more corrupt and riddled with problems than that of Great Britain prior to the introduction of the postage stamp. For example, if you wanted to mail a newspaper—theoretically your right—you needed to provide a penny tip for the service as an unspoken bribe. A second penny tip was necessary to receive mail early. The postman delivered the mail to everyone, but they would make special early rounds only for those who had given them extra money.

There were also fees added to letters based on the time of day they were mailed. One fee was charged for letters mailed between 6:00 P.M. and 7:00 A.M. the following day. A higher fee was added for letters mailed between 7:00 A.M. and 7:30 A.M., and still another charge was added for letters brought to the post office between 7:30 A.M. and 7:45 A.M.

Numerous other charges applied. Letters might have one price for being sent 15 miles, with extra charges added for additional mileage. A price of 4d (4 pence) might take your letter to a spot within easy walking distance of your own home, while a letter sent 400 miles away might cost 13d, even though the weight was identical.

Even the term "letter" was defined so as to provide extra revenue. One sheet of paper was a "letter." If you wanted to place that paper in an envelope, the envelope was a second or "double" letter requiring twice the money. This system was taken to such an extreme that, if it was applied to current business practices, a business person sending a one-page letter and his or her business card in an envelope would pay a triple rate.

Book manuscripts and other large-volume shipping needs were prohibitively costly. The rate was based on each page being a letter, so private messengers had to be employed.

It was not necessary to prepay postage. You could send a person a letter and require the receiver to pay. This meant that if someone applied for a job in one community, then returned to a second community for a short period of time, he might not be able to afford the postage for a letter notifying him that he had the job. Many people went months without learning important information concerning family problems, friends who were sick or had died, and other personal needs because they could not afford the postage due.

Methods for cheating the post office were also devised. For example, a pair of lovers would send a letter to each other with either code words or code spelling on the envelope. A letter addressed to James B. Rathborn might be his sweetheart's way of saying she would be coming to visit. A letter addressed to J. B. Rathborn might be their code for "I love you." Enough people used code messages on the envelopes, which the postman had to show to the recipient before he or she decided to accept and pay, that substantial sums were lost.

The honest poor were the ones who suffered most under this system. A person receiving a letter who was too poor to pay for it might have to let it sit in the post office for a period of time. If he or she could still not come up with the money, it would be returned. Thus families were kept incommunicado and opportunities for financial betterment were lost because the letter providing this chance was returned when the recipient could not afford the postage.

The cost of the postage can best be understood in terms of daily income. The average poor person led a bare existence on 18 pence a day. Many letters cost 6 pence, so receiving a single letter could eliminate a third of a day's income.

In 1837, Sir Rowland Hill wrote a pamphlet supporting the idea of low postage, paid in advance. Letters would be charged a set rate regardless of how many sheets of paper were involved. A charge by weight might be practical, but Hill showed how different-weight envelopes could contain the same number of pages, depending upon the paper used.

Hill felt that there should be a single penny rate for all letters mailed throughout England. He wanted prepaid letters to have special envelopes printed with the postage amount. However, a Dundee bookshop owner named James Chalmers thought that adhesive-backed stamps would be better.

In 1839, a design contest was held to create the first postage stamp. There were four first prizes of 100 pounds each awarded to the best of the 2,600 entries. That sum was extremely large, yet none of the award-winning designs were retained. Instead, Hill took matters into his own hands and created the Penny Black, a simple stamp with the bust of Queen Victoria. The best was a direct copy of a commemorative medal made by William Wyon and popular with the Queen.

Hill used watercolors for the design. The engravers Charles and Frederic Heath handled the tooling needed before the engraving was sent to Perkins, Bacon and Co. for printing.

ONE PENNY BLACK

On May 2, 1840, at least three of the prepared postage stamps were used on letters. The one-penny rate for mail sent throughout England had been in effect since early January, but these were the first stamps to be carried. The official release date came on May 6 and the stamps were immensely popular.

The 1840 One Penny with the design concept that made prepaid postage a reality.

The idea that letters could be sent anywhere in England for a penny intrigued the public. One description of the response was written approximately May 8 stated:

"People now rush to pay postage as they rush to the pit for a theatre on a crowded night. During the last half hour at the principal offices, the force for taking in letters is far overtaxed. . . . The great hall at St. Martin's-le-Grand was nearly

The 1841 Penny Black.

filled with the spectators, marshalled in a line by the police, to watch the crowds pressing, scuffling and fighting to get first to the window. Formerly one window sufficed to receive letters. On this evening six windows, with two receivers at each, were bombarded by applicants. As the last quarter-hour approached and the crowd still thickened, a seventh window was opened, and that none might be turned away, Mr. Bokenham made some other opening and took in letters and money himself. . . . No one failed to get his letter in; more than 3,000 were posted there that evening between 5 and 6 P.M. When the window closed, the mob, delighted at the energy displayed by the officers, gave one cheer for the Post Office and another for Rowland Hill.''

There was a side ''business'' created by the new penny post. Numerous illustrators made special envelopes to hold letters under the new system. Some were covered with symbolic designs and elaborate artwork. Others were satirical in nature. They were such a novelty that the *London Times* often reviewed the new items for sale.

One particular review concerned the work of a 15-year-old artist named Richard Doyle who was working for a printing company making envelopes. Doyle would later become a top illustrator for the humor magazine *Punch*. The *Times* review stated, in part:

''Everybody has, we presume, before this time, had an opportunity of examining those very extraordinary specimens of British Art—the penny post envelopes. On the merits of design for those absurdities we have never heard but one opinion. From Sir Robert Peel down to the lowest kitchen wench the new covers have been laughed at by every man, woman and child of the community who has the slightest perception of the ludicrous. Anything more ridiculous could hardly be imagined, and in consequence the caricaturists have done their best to show up these monstrous and universally circulating libels upon the public taste. In this laudable exercise of ingenuity Mr. Fores certainly takes the lead; and we have just been favoured with a sight of a batch of envelopes published by him relating to a variety of subjects, which, in point of execution, are far superior, but which, although intended to amuse, are, we are bound to say, as regards design, far less likely to create laughter than their great prototypes. Mr. Fores's envelopes relate to hunting, courting, racing, dancing, coaching and music, and are all excellently humorous in their respective ways. We recommend those who buy post-office envelopes merely for fun—we suppose few purchase them with any other object—to purchase Mr. Fores's envelopes instead. They are better and more amusing, both in design and execution, and are certainly more creditable to the public taste.''

The fascination with stamps and prepaid postage was high but not so high as to avoid numerous problems. The wealthy would send servants to prepay letters being mailed to friends. The servants pocketed the money in some instances, then sent the letters with postage due as in the past, a fact never mentioned to their employers. The recipients were equally wealthy and never thought that theft of funds had occurred.

The stamps were considered close to legal tender. Many people would use the prepaid but unused postage as small change. However, when bars and other businesses refused the stamps, it was not because they were a different form of "money." It was almost always because the person to whom the stamps were presented had never seen the colorful bits of paper.

Many people took postage stamps as a matter of prestige, buying more than they needed to make an impression. The British publication *Chamber's Journal* ran a story that was typical of what was happening. It concerned a sailor who stopped into a post office while his ship was in the harbor. The sailor needed just a penny stamp for a letter to his friend. However, he bought five shillings' worth of stamps because they were more impressive and he felt he owed his friend something special.

The Penny Black was a brilliant idea but a poor color choice. The cancellation mark seemed to disappear, making it possible for someone to use a stamp twice. It was decided to change the coloring to a brownish-red.

The One Penny stamp, as well as a Two Pence blue-colored stamp of similar design for heavier letters, were instant successes. At the end of the first year, at least one woman decided to use the stamps for decorations. She advertised for them in the *London Times*, announcing her intention to use them to paper her walls. They were used, abused, saved by some, and discarded by others. However, so many were made that, even today, approximately 1½ centuries later, the stamps are in the $200 range for an average used copy.

The One Penny Red is far more common than the Two Penny Blue but comes in numerous varieties. There were corner check letters added to the stamps to reduce the problem of counterfeiting. The letters vary with the position of the stamp on the printing plate to such a degree that it would take 240 different Penny Reds to have all varieties in your collection. Collectors who can afford them may make a British specialty collection of the Penny Reds to the exclusion of all other stamps.

The earliest British postage stamps were printed unperforated. They had to be cut apart with scissors. As a result, the early stamps are often found with oddly cut surfaces.

It was August of 1841 when a variation of the printing process was suggested. This would leave lines scored between the stamps so that they could be more easily separated. The concept was rejected, as was an idea six years later which required special blades to roulette the stamps. The rouletting process leaves many tiny cuts in the paper making separation easy.

The perforation issue was debated, but meanwhile other stamps were being issued. These all were embossed with the Queen's head and had denominations ranging from one shilling (1847 issue) to six pence (1854), with a 10-pence stamp appearing in 1848.

The printing quality of these early British stamps is quite poor. Often there was an overlapping design. Obtaining quality examples with good margins around the design is almost impossible. The designs were also octagonal, so many of the users, who were forced to cut the then unperforated issues, would also damage the stamps by cutting them to the octagonal shape. Quality examples are almost nonexistent and usually far more expensive than the first postage stamps of England.

The embossed stamps, which comprised these early British issues, are readily available today in a slightly different form. The same embossing was done for postal stationery—envelopes with the stamps printed on them for sale by the Post Offices. Many collectors and dealers with a larcenous bent to their character like to sell as originals the same stamp designs clipped from the more readily available envelopes. Fortunately, there is a difference you can spot.

The British printers were concerned with possible counterfeiting. They used paper having dual threads running through it when printing the regular postage stamps, something that was not done with the embossed postal stationery. If the threads are missing from the stamps offered for sale, they are not the stamps but the stamped portion of the envelopes that have been removed.

The 6-pence stamp, the last to be issued among the first seven designs created in those early years, did not have the silk threads. However, counterfeit detection was possible because a watermarked paper was used. This paper has the letters "V.R." visible, again a situation *not* done with the envelopes.

One of the problems the British Post Office faced during its early years was the common one of people clipping pieces from postage stamps and making new ones. A stamp might be cancelled in the upper corner, with the lower section untouched. Another stamp might have the reverse situation. By cutting and fitting the pieces, you could mail a letter with the two cancellation-free pieces of already canceled stamps.

The British developed the idea of adding letters to the four corners of their postage stamps. The letters would be reversed from top to bottom, making it difficult for people to use portions of the uncanceled stamps. This was done for the first time in 1857, but by 1864, the One Penny stamp with the letters was even more sophisticated. The plate numbers used for the printing were in the scrolls on either side of the head of Queen Victoria. It was possible to collect by letter position, plate number, and other ways, including with the various cancellation marks. This has great appeal for those collectors more interested in printing and cancellation variations than original design. Some of the plate numbers are scarce, but most of the varieties can be collected even with a low budget.

The perforated stamps were introduced in 1854. This was a boon for collectors as well because perforations allowed stamp separation with less risk of accidentally destroying the stamps.

Great Britian saw no need for varying stamp designs in those early years. There were numerous collectors, but the collecting public was not important to the Post Office. The greatest concern was with moving the mail under the new system and this did not require radical changes in design. Only more efficient printing and separating techniques were of interest. Thus the 1841 One Penny stamp, with only slight variations in design, remained in use until the perforated versions of stamps were introduced.

In 1864, a One Penny stamp showing the Queen's head once again was introduced. She became almost ageless, the stamp being used for the next sixteen years without major changes.

The British were very concerned about the reuse of their stamps. In addition to the letters at the corners, they also experimented with printing and inks. The De LaRue Company, a major printer of security paper (paper used for items where counterfeiting could be a serious problem), developed a method of surface printing with an ink which would run when removal was attempted. The erasing of the cancellation mark would result in the elimination of the stamp design, proving the attempted fraud and preventing the stamp from being used.

Surface-printed 4-pence stamps were attempted in 1855 and continued for seven years. Then, in 1862, a variation of the concept was tried with the 3-pence, 6-pence, 9-pence, and 1-shilling issues. The 4-pence stamps were redesigned, but the printing technique remained similar.

The 9-pence stamp is probably the most desired from this period. It was a stamp meant to cover the cost of long-distance postage. Envelopes containing these stamps traveled to Asia, South America and elsewhere. Many Australian collectors seek envelopes with these stamps since Australia was one of the British colonies where the letters were received. Most are poorly centered and somewhat damaged from the handling in transit, yet so rare that they are extremely desirable.

The collector of the stamps of Great Britain has a wide variety of postmarks and cancellations from which to choose. The earliest One Penny stamps often had a Maltese Cross for the cancellation mark. Later, as the stamps were used to send mail throughout the vast British Empire, numerous cancellations occurred, including those with different cities of origin.

Britain had what might be called branch post offices located in such areas as Thailand, Chile, Gibraltar, and elsewhere. These were not post offices for these countries. The country would have its own postal service separate from this. Instead, these were part of the British system and were designated by a code. A letter and two digits used in the cancellation of a regular British stamp would indicate that the stamp was used in a foreign country by a British branch post office. Thus a stamp with a cancellation such as C51 (St. Thomas) indicates a British Post Office branch. A cancellation with just three digits and no letters would indicate that the stamp was used by the country's own post office system. Once the countries began issuing their own stamps, the three-digit cancellations were no longer essential.

Britain not only led the way in producing the postage stamp, it also pioneered high mailing rates. A 5-shilling stamp was introduced in 1867 as a business use stamp. Exporters often needed expensive postage and the 5-shilling stamp was meant to reduce the amount of paper which had to be applied to packages. The equivalent stamp in American money would have cost approximately \$1.30, a substantial portion of a man's daily wage. However, this was only the forerunner of the 5-pound stamp of 1882, a stamp the equivalent of a week's high pay for the average American. To put together equal postage in the United States would cost \$26. However, these stamps are not as rare as you might think. They were such a curiosity and so impressive when received on a package that most people saved them. If a company receiving a package from abroad had no interest in the stamps, one of the low-level employees would retain the wrappings because the stamp represented such a large sum of money. Thus even today it is often easier to locate an example of a British high-value stamp than to find a more widely printed low-value from the same period.

There is a difference between the way Americans and British collectors seek the British postal issues, especially the stamps from the early years. Most American collectors are interested in the most colorful of the stamps, their desire is more for the variations in design than anything else. The British collectors enjoy the subtle shading differences on the same designs, finding an appeal in the slight vagaries of the printer's art.

Today the stamps of Great Britain are among the most desired in the world. Arabs concerned with protecting their money after oil runs out frequently buy collections of great worth and predictable future desirability. British rarities are often the stamps of choice for them. Other collectors delight in the historic aspects of the country as it is connected with the modern postal system. Whatever the personal interest, this is an excellent field for the collector.

7

Canadian Stamps

Collectors of Canadian stamps enter a special world of philately. This is a country whose history is tied with three separate nations. The French explored the northern regions and were responsible for much of the fur trade for which early Canada is so famous. Even today, Quebec considers French to be the primary language and Quebec nationalists feel that they should have a separate, French culture-oriented country.

England settled the lower sections during the period when there was colonization throughout North America. The country is part of the British Commonwealth and England's royal family is extremely important.

The United States is also closely related to Canada. In part, this is because of family ties among residents of both nations. The early British settlers often made their way to both areas, so within one family, some members ended up in what is now Toronto, while others may have gone to what is now New York, Detroit, or elsewhere. In the Far West, Vancouver is closely linked with Washington State. Many families have relatives in both areas as well as ancestors whose homes originally were in England.

What all this means to collectors is that there is far greater interest in Canadian stamps than in the stamps of most other countries. Collectors of both United States and British Commonwealth issues feel close ties with Canada. Events commemorated on Canadian stamps also will often have interest to collectors in many nations. In fact, the first postage stamps of Canada were printed by a New York firm and focused on subjects ranging from the Queen to the Canadian beaver. The latter was the economic symbol of the country since the sale of beaver pelts for hats, coats, and other uses was a major source of income.

The first Canadian issues included a 3-pence stamp (Scott # 1) featuring the beaver design, a stamp which was most commonly used for postage, a 6-pence Prince Albert issue, (Scott # 2) and a 12-pence Queen Victoria design. It is the Victoria issue which is the most valuable because so few were printed or needed. Unlike England, Canada did relatively little business overseas where high-value postage was needed. The people were more likely to import goods through the mails than to export them.

The first stamps were printed on what was known as "laid" paper, an approach changed in 1852 to a type of paper known as "wove." This is because laid paper fails to hold the design effectively. Thus the early stamps are often quite light and the first cancellation marks, usually a group of concentric circles looking like a target, were not always effective.

There are several distinctly different papers used for the wove process as the Canadian government experimented. The 1851 stamps did not adhere well to the envelopes, so this was another problem to be overcome.

By 1855, rate changes were necessary in Canada because of the British connection. Letters going to Europe through the British packet system had to have a 10-pence stamp. Another stamp design was created to allow for payment in different monetary systems, the stamp (Scott # 9) sold at 6½-pence sterling or 7½-pence currency. There was also a very common ½-penny Queen Victoria stamp, which is a great rarity today. Vast numbers of the ½-penny issue were used with newspaper wrappers and the majority of them were torn by people opening their papers.

It was 1858 when the Canadians added a perforating machine to their stamp production. However, instead of just perforating all their stamps, they would perforate on special order for a charge of 5 cents per 1,000 stamps. This was because the machine was so crude, the stamps could only be perforated in one direction. The sheets had to be run through twice to cover both horizontal and vertical perforation needs.

Canada went strictly on the decimal currency system in 1859, a system which again linked it more fully with the system in the United States. The new stamps bore denominations of 1 cent, 10 cents, 12½ cents, and 17 cents (Scott # 14–19).

Once again there were experiments with the issues and numerous variations in printings. A total of 25 different color shades exist for the 10-cent stamp alone. Some, such as the black-brown shade, are extremely rare. Others are relatively common, though few are well centered.

Canada was in a constant state of political change and this fact was reflected by its stamps. The British North American Act resulted in the creation of the Dominion of Canada which united several formerly independent areas such as Quebec, New Brunswick, and Nova Scotia. This was in 1867 and, two years later, the land owned by the Hudson's Bay Company was purchased. Then, in 1871, with British Columbia added, Canada took the ocean-to-ocean appearance it has today. Naturally new stamps had to be issued.

Queen Victoria dominated the first stamps of the Dominion in 1868, her portrait so large in comparison with previous stamp designs that these issues are known as the Large Queens. A reduced-size version, the "Small Queens," were substituted in 1870 to reduce paper needs. These were the first stamps to follow the rather dull British design concept instead of having the commemorative flexibility used with the beaver and Prince Albert issues.

Among the more desirable versions of these issues are the watermarked Large Queens (not all the Large Queens were on watermarked paper) and some of the shade versions of the less expensive Small Queens. A number of the Small Queens are also known with double transfers, the duplication of a portion of the design caused by an imperfect die.

In 1897 the printing was improved by a contract between the Canadian Post Office and the American Bank Note Company. The latter was one of the most skilled of the United States high-security printers. The company produced postage stamps, paper money, stocks, bonds, and similar items that needed protection from counterfeiting. Since the contract did not relate to either a British or Canadian printer, one stipulation was that the American Bank Note Company handle the work on Canadian soil.

THE JUBILEE STAMPS

The 1897 stamps are the Jubilee issues representing the first sixty years of the reign of Queen Victoria (Scott # 50-65). They were meant to be sold to collectors to raise money for the government, not just for use as postage. A broad range of values, from 1 cent to $5, were printed for sale. The stamps were of a rectangular design, which would have a similar appeal to that of the Columbian Exposition Commemoratives of 1893. Those American stamps were saved in such large quantities that profits well in excess of costs were made by the government.

The Jubilee stamps did well for the time, but there was no great demand for the higher-value issues. The government forgot that the identical design for all the stamps (a young head of Victoria shown full face and an older head shown in profile) might not be so appealing as the varied images on the Columbians. Today it will cost approximately $1,000 for a set of the lower-value mint Jubilee issues of 1897 and a few thousand dollars for the high values. Yet this is still several thousand dollars less than the prices for the similarly scarce Columbians.

The standard 1897–1898 issue (Scott # 66–73) featured maple leaves in the corners of each stamp as well as Victoria's head. They are rather unattractive and, like all stamps with the denomination not the design changed, rather boring. However, they represent a changing era in Canadian and British history as well as one of the final years of Victoria's lengthy (64 years in all) reign.

A variation of the maple leaf stamps occurred the following year when the lower portion of the stamps had numerals added to reflect the denomination.

The most desirable stamps remaining relatively affordable for that period is what amounts to a multiple commemorative issue in 1898 (Scott # 85–86). The 2-cent stamp itself shows a map of the world and is printed in three colors—it honored the British Empire and had as a slogan "We Hold A Vaster Empire Than Has Been." Also printed on the stamp is "Xmas 1898," the first stamp to be specifically noted as a Christmas issue.

The postage stamp of the 1898 Christmas issue is directly tied in with Britain for a stronger reason. The members of the British Commonwealth gathered together to lower their postage rates. They decided to jointly begin charging the equivalent of one British penny as the base rate beginning Christmas Day. This translated to 2 cents for the base postage in Canada (1-cent Canadian was equal to ½-British penny).

Queen Victoria's death in 1901 resulted in a change to stamps featuring Edward VII, the first issues coming in 1903. All first year of issues of this type are popular and the Edward VII stamps are no exception. The high-value issues (10 cents, 20 cents, 50 cents) are greatly prized by collectors today, especially those in mint condition.

The next break came in 1908 when the designs took on a fascinating display of Canadian history. The Quebec Tercentenary Issues (Scott # 96–103) do include some portraits, such as the Prince and Princess of Wales (½-cent stamp), Jacques Cartier and Samuel Champlain (1-cent issue), King Edward and Queen Alexandra (2-cent issue) and, on the 7-cent issue, Generals Wolfe and Montcalm. However, it is the other issues that offer variety. The 5-cent issue shows Samuel Champlain's fortlike home in Quebec, an interesting rendering of a historic dwelling. The 10-cent stamp is a view of the city of Quebec as it appeared in 1700. This was a French fortified structure along the water, reproduced in such detail that only with high magnification can you see all the ships, the windows in the buildings, and other details. This is quite a change in printing and engraving skill from the original Canadian issues.

The 15-cent stamp shows Champlain's departure for the West. Indians are loading canoes and facial details are excellent despite more than a dozen people being drawn on each small stamp.

The highest denomination, the 20-cent yellow brown stamp, shows the arrival of Cartier and his ships at Quebec. This series is extremely popular and represents a radical new interest for Canadian collectors of the day. Such commemorative designs had been popular in the United States but were ignored until then by Canadian designers.

Other issues followed. A design similar to the one found on the American $2 bill is seen on the 1917 stamp of Canada. This 2-cent issue shows the Quebec Conference of 1867. It is a room filled with the political leaders and again reflects both detail and a paralleling of history.

The Canadian postal commemoratives that began to flow from the printing presses spent less time honoring the royal family and more time highlighting the history of Canada. Important buildings have been shown—Memorial Hall, Garry Gate, Chateau Ramezay, the Parliament Buildings, Confederation Memorial, and others. There have been symbolic representations of Niagara Falls, the Royal Canadian Mounted Police, the paper industry, the advancing railroad, and the like. Birds, sporting events, Canadian Indians and their heritage, and numerous other subjects also have been shown.

The result of all this is that from 1908 on Canadian issues have featured a cross-section of designs touching on almost everyone's interest. Typical are the current issues released in 1983. Commonwealth Day is being celebrated with the first $5 stamp to be released since the 1897 Jubilee issue. The stamp not only has historic value, it also adds a much needed issue for large mailers as well as an interesting collectible. It will not feature the Queen, as did the earlier issue, but will show Point Pelee National Park which is located on Lake Erie, across from the American state of Ohio. The park, in Ontario near Leamington, is the national park farthest south in the country and a popular location for bird-watchers.

Canada, like most countries, has issues tied in with special United Nations themes. Since 1983 is the World Communications Year, a 30-cent stamp honored the event.

In April of 1983, various artifacts from Canada's history were featured on four different values of stamps. Other issues for that year alone include a stamp honoring Sir Humphrey Gilbert, the navigator who helped claim Newfoundland for England; Cure Labelle, who was for fifty-eight years the nineteenth-century founder of 60 villages north of Montréal; and even Josiah Henson (1789–1883), a fugitive slave who helped a group of ex-slaves found a cooperative settlement near Dresden, Ontario.

Within just the one year, you can find stamps honoring the Canadian Army and militia, stamps showing early steam locomotives which made their way across the land, the hundredth anniversary of the discovery of nickel at Sudbury, Ontario, commemoratives for the World University Games in Edmonton, Alta, and others.

Sometimes the Canadian stamps have extremely dramatic themes. An April 13, 1982, issue for the Marathon of Hope is probably the most unusual in Canada's postal history because of the man to whom it was dedicated. This was Terry Fox, a youth who died of cancer in June 1981. Fox, although he had already lost a leg to cancer and knew he was dying from the disease, ran across almost the entire nation in order to raise money for cancer research. He did not quite go coast to coast before he became too ill to carry on, but his run and his subsequent death was one of the most heroic acts of the twentieth century.

Among other issues are those featuring national parks, aircraft, and transportation. Canada Day is regularly commemorated, the June 1982 celebration resulting in the issue of a dozen different designs from featuring paintings selected from each of the ten provinces and two territories. The Salvation Army has been featured, events in history and of course, the Royal Family. It is thus an exciting, extremely varied area for every collector.

8

Collecting Other Foreign Stamps

Because this book is meant to be an introduction to stamp collecting, attempting to discuss the postal issues of many of the countries of the world is impossible. Chapter 9 discusses some highly specialized collectibles, such as those issued by the tiny nation of Bhutan. But for now, let us briefly look at the reasons why collectors seek the issues of any number of countries.

Stamps tell the story of a nation, its changing politics and rulers. Many of the stamps you see come from countries that probably did not exist when you were born. Wars, revolution, the granting of independence to what had been a colonial nation—all can lead to changes in name.

Most collectors of postage stamps from countries other than their own do so because of a common heritage. Americans are interested in the stamps of Great Britain because of the strong historical tie. Yet many Americans have ancestors who came from Poland or Spain, Germany or Italy, and they maintain an interest in their "roots." This is often an incentive to collect postage stamps from abroad.

Religion can also be a philatelic factor. Many Catholics start collecting Vatican issues, then expand into related countries, such as Italy and, most recently, Poland. Jews first may be interested in the stamps of Israel, then expand to nations of the Middle East. Whatever your ancestry, you may find that collecting particular stamps has an appeal for you.

Sometimes the collection evolves for other reasons. A nation may be so new that you can afford a complete range of its postal issues. Or you might encounter a tiny country with a long history

These Israeli stamps appeal to both theater buffs and to those interested in Israel.

that is totally unfamiliar to you. Curiosity is a strong motivating factor with the latter.

Another possibility is to limit your collection to stamps of the world as it existed during a certain period in history. There are collections of stamps of countries that only existed prior to World War II. There are also collections limited to the years during World War II, many of the stamps being specially printed as countries that were overrun by other nations.

The more politically important a country, and the more it needs hard currency from other nations, the more likely it is to issue large quantities of different stamp designs each year. Russia, for example, seldom issues fewer than 125 different commemoratives in any one year. Obviously, the Russian people are not striking against the mail service because they can not get

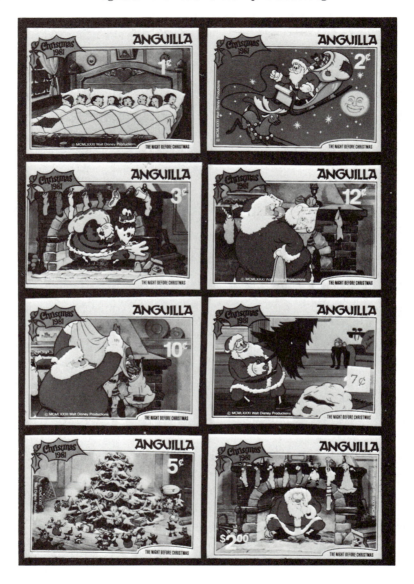

The stamps of Anguilla are very popular with many beginning collectors. Often, such stamps are sold for extremely high prices to take advantage of the immediate interest in new issues. However, because these stamps are relatively common and printed in large numbers, the price drops quickly; subsequently the resale value is limited.

These stamps from the Turks and Caicos Islands, part of the British Commonwealth, not only show the physical location of the island but also depict some of the unique features tourists may encounter.

enough commemoratives. The people of every country will send their mail with the stamps available, even if the designs go unchanged for years, as happened in both England and the United

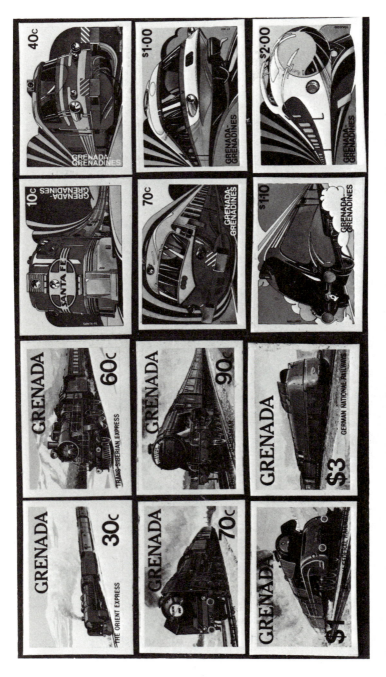

There are many ways to collect topicals related to history and countries. One approach is to collect stamps which show images of the various kinds of transportation that have been—or still are—used to move the mail. Included in this kind of collection might be these inexpensive stamps from Grenada.

More popular stamps from Anguilla.

States when postage stamps were first introduced. The motivation behind so many issues is profit. Unfortunately, this means that you must lay out large sums of money if you are seeking a complete collection.

Bhutan, discussed in the next chapter, is the rare country which admits that it uses stamps for income. However, their issues are often so unusual that no one cares. Most serious collectors, though, will choose to stay as much as possible with countries that do not abuse the number of issues released.

You might find that contrary to conventional "wisdom," your taste runs to such stamp-issuing countries as the Arab emirates (nicknamed "the Sand Dunes"), which issue far more stamps than internal need demands. You might like the designs and consider the items collectible, even though others feel they are only fund-raisers for the government. If this is the case, the easiest way to avoid getting taken too badly is not to buy the current issues. Most of these countries issue high-value denominations seldom used by the public. These are purchased by many collectors, then resold to dealers at a substantial loss within a few months. Buying them secondhand can save you a fortune over the new-issue price, and they can all be obtained in mint, never-hinged condition.

If you go to school, you might want to concentrate on countries that interest you in world history. Some new student collectors specialize in one country a semester, combining their hobby with what they are learning, often matching stamps commemorating people and events with their current studies. Then, after exploring several areas, they specialize in just one for the next few years, attempting to obtain as complete a collection as they can.

However you choose to expand, foreign stamps will take you into a different culture, a unique history, and often help you learn a new language. They can make people thousands of miles away seem like next-door neighbors. This opportunity is yet another reason why your new hobby can be so exciting.

9

Special Collecting

There are many special areas whose stamps you may enjoy collecting. Some of these countries have hundreds of thousands of philatelists interested in them—the United States is one. Others are simply little oddball states, such as Bhutan. Whatever the case, specialized collecting opens new vistas of hobby pleasure.

AIR MAIL

He was impatient as he waited. The mail was late. He had been told that the message would be sent by air to speed the service, but you could never trust the mails these days.

There would be a good excuse for the delay. The winds were bad. A storm came up. This was the fastest service available, yet the sun was beginning to set and there was no sign of the message.

Suddenly he saw it soaring through the sky. It was coming in, landing perfectly, the message attached near its leg.

Near its leg? Air mail? Yes, and the man who was waiting lived more than 2,000 years ago. He was a Chinese gentleman and the air mail he was seeking was a pigeon trained to carry messages.

Contrary to what you might have imagined, pigeons are among the oldest conveyers of mail the world has ever known. You might say that bird-delivery started with the Great Flood of the Bible, if you consider the olive branch brought in the beak of a dove. However, regular message service using swallows or homing pigeons was known to the ancient Chinese, the Greeks, and the Romans. The Persians and Arabs also had air mail. It was a way to have messages sent long distance without an enemy being able to detect them. Even when the birds flew over lines of soldiers, the enemy lacked the weapons to shoot the birds from the skies. They were also unable to determine which birds had messages, thus camouflaging their messengers. Pigeons were used extensively in Jerusalem. The Crusaders who fought in the Holy Land learned of this method and took the information to other parts of Europe.

During the siege of Paris in 1870–71, the Parisians were desperately attempting to get mail to the outside world. Homing pigeons fly in only one direction—toward their home. Birds in Paris could not be trained to go elsewhere and birds living away from that city could not be trained to land where desired. The answer was to utilize several new forms of technology, including photography and aeronautics—actually balloons.

BALLOON MAIL

Hot-air balloons were invented at the end of the eighteenth-century. The Montgolfier Brothers were among the pioneers, with a man named Blanchard credited with first using a balloon to carry a letter. This occurred in 1785 in Philadelphia when George Washington gave him a message for the flight.

The first serious effort to achieve balloon mail is believed to have taken place in 1859; when John Wise took letters bound for New York City from St. Louis in his balloon *The Atlantic.*

The Paris situation mentioned earlier required a serious gamble. Ballooning was a popular activity and the Parisians knew that the Prussian Army which surrounded the city would not have an easy time shooting down the balloons. The air currents were such that balloons could leave the city but might have difficulty returning. Thus it was decided to pack balloons with homing pigeons, which could be used to return messages.

The first successful launch occurred in September 23, 1870, the balloon landing 65 miles away. Both passengers and pigeons were involved in the flights, the majority avoiding the enemy. A total of 384 pigeons made the trip, along with 21 tons of mail.

The one dramatic reminder of carrier-pigeon mail came when 5,000 birds were released during the First World Postage Stamp Exhibition in Prague in 1962. These pigeons had peace messages and were a fascinating reminder of an unusual type of mail.

Collectors of postal history are today more likely to find

stamps commemorating pigeons than examples of the early messages often contained on a kind of early microfilm. The most readily available postal items from the early days of air mail are represented by the balloon mail.

Many countries have issued stamps relating to these early experiments with airborne communication. Typical are such stamps as the 1949 U.S. 15-cent air mail featuring doves circling the globe while carrying messages (Scott #C42) and the 1959 7-cent air mail (Scott #C54), which celebrated the 100th anniversary of the launch of the mail-carrying balloon *Jupiter*. The latter traveled between Lafayette and Crawfordsville, Indiana.

ZEPPELINS

Lighter-than-air flight was a reality for almost a century when serious efforts were being made to create a more controlled balloon flight. These experiments created rather awkward craft that did not have long-range or heavy-payload potential. The first heavier-than-air machine, designed by Orville and Wilbur Wright and successfully flown at Kitty Hawk, North Carolina, in December 1903, also seemed impractical. Some visionaries saw tremendous opportunity for the future but many immediate problems of distance and control were not being resolved.

The answer, when it came, evolved from Count Ferdinand von Zeppelin, a soldier with the German cavalry. He defied conventional balloon design by reworking the frame into a giant oval with a metal frame which could hold hydrogen.

The first ship, known as the *Z-1*, was flown in 1900, then grounded as being unsafe. A change in the design resulted in a more efficient engine and safer design, but the *Z-2* could not handle inclement weather. It was not until 1906 that the third design, the *Z-3*, proved that Zeppelin's theories were practical. A dozen people flew 2½ hours in his ship on a controlled flight of 70 miles. By 1908, with further improvements, the Zeppelin Company was organized and the new "blimps," as they came to be known in America, were put into production for serious commercial use.

Zeppelin flights almost always involved the carrying of mail. The quantity of letters varied with each flight. Most of the covers marked as being for Zeppelin post were flown after World War I. The covers flown before that time are quite valuable by comparison.

Perfectly centered examples of uncanceled Zeppelin stamps. These stamps are of continual interest to collectors and investors, in part because of their history and the history of the *Zeppelin*. The Zeppelins are the only expensive items needed to assemble a complete collection of U.S. airmail stamps.

The United States Post Office issued three of the most controversial and desired air mail stamps in 1930. Air mail postage stamps had been issued since 1918 but the 1930 were specially for use with the planned European–Pan American round-trip flight of the *Graf Zeppelin* in April of that year. These stamps, known in the Scott Catalog as #C13, C14, and C15, cost $4.55 for a complete set. The high cost, both for using this mail service and for the strong collector interest anticipated, was expected to bring large profits to everyone involved. Instead, the cost was discouraging to collectors and many of the stamps went unsold. These were eventually destroyed, greatly reducing the number available today. The remaining stamps, especially if in perfect condition, are highly valued and quite costly. Since the Zeppelin image is popular with collectors throughout the world, the market is much broader than for other air mail stamps.

In 1936, what was to be the ultimate lighter-than-air craft came from the Zeppelin factory. This was the magnificent

Hindenburg, designed to be the ultimate luxury liner of the sky. Tragically, it became to dirigibles what the *Andrea Dorea* was to cruise ships—a disaster.

The *Hindenburg* could fly for 9,000 miles without having to refuel, and its top speed was 90 miles an hour. The dirigible, which was 810 feet long and capable of holding 42,000 pounds of cargo, was kept aloft with hydrogen—which would prove its undoing.

The popularity of air flight, the Zeppelin ships and the *Hindenburg* especially can be seen by the first North American flight it made. It coincided with the Third International Philatelic Exhibition in New York which went from May 9 to 17, 1937. The exhibition was held in the Grand Central Palace in New York and covers were flown on the *Hindenburg* across the Atlantic Ocean, the first such Zeppelin mail delivery.

American Airlines established an airdrome in New York specifically for the *Hindenburg* flights and the U.S. Post Office maintained an area to process the Zeppelin mail. Everything went smoothly until May 6, 1937, when the *Hindenburg* approached the airdrome at 7:00 P.M. Approximately 20 minutes later, an explosion shook the handling facility. By the time the foreman could see what was happening, the giant airship was in flames. No one was allowed near the flaming wreckage and it was assumed that everything on board would be destroyed. Miraculously, 357 pieces of mail survived in various stages of being charred by the flames. These envelopes were highly prized "crash covers" and the collection of these as well as other disaster survivors has become popular with many air mail enthusiasts.

The crash of the *Hindenburg* ended the serious consideration of dirigibles as mail or passenger carriers. Even if they could be equipped with helium instead of hydrogen, they were too slow compared with the dramatic changes in flight. In fact, by then the air mail service by planes was well established.

SCHEDULED AIR MAIL

If you ever see a large collection of air mail history, you may spot some postcards from Nantes in 1910. These are marked *"Par aeroplane"* but never left the ground. Many of the early experimental flights which followed the Wright Brothers' successful effort did have letters or cards carried for friends. However, these are fairly rare.

Air parcel post did begin in 1910 even if letter carrying had not truly started. The honor of sending the first package by air, officially recognized through cards issued to commemorate the event, goes to the Morehouse Martens Company, which sent a package of silk from Dayton, Ohio, to nearby Columbus, Ohio, by airplane.

Regular air delivery of mail is credited to the city of Allahabad in what was then British India. Sir Walter Wyndham arranged for air service with special cards and letters to be used. These bore postmarks rather than stamps to denote the service. The year was 1911, and Wyndham's concept was adopted by the United States on an experimental basis in both Garden City, New York, and Fort Smith, Arkansas. Italy also inaugurated service between Milan and Turin and an air delivery of newspapers was tried in Morocco, the paper traveling from Casablanca to both Rabat and Fez.

Italy is credited with the first air mail stamps. Regular flights were inaugurated experimentally in 1917. Service was established between Rome and Turin, and between Naples and Palermo in an effort to determine cost, demand and feasibility. Special delivery stamps were overprinted to handle the air mail charges.

Meanwhile, the United States was printing its first postal issues featuring the Curtis Jenny Biplane which would be used in 1918 (Scott #C1-3). Two years earlier, Congress established a fund to experiment with the creation of an air mail service. The major population centers were to be the first recipients of this system, the maiden flight being a New York to Philadelphia to Washington, D.C. linkup. What no one realized was that the inaugural event would be more in the nature of a comedy more appropriate to the movies.

On May 15, 1918, the United States Post Office, in cooperation with the U.S. Army, prepared a special ceremony for the inaugural flight. A Curtiss JN-4-H biplane, the *Jenny*, with specially modified cabin, was loaded with mail and taken to the polo ground in Washington, D.C. President Woodrow Wilson, the postmaster-general, various congressmen and others spoke of the wonders of the day. Wilson then personally handed the pilot, Lt. George Boyle, a letter addressed to the postmaster of New York. Boyle saluted, climbed into his plane, and was unable to start the engine. He was out of gas before he could get started.

Aviation may have advanced tremendously since the Wright Brothers flight, but that did not mean that airplane fuel was readily available. There was no way to gas up. After much discussion, men were dispatched to all nearby aircraft with orders to drain enough fuel from them to fill the tank of Lt. Boyle's plane.

Finally everything was ready. The engine started, the propeller blade turned, and Lt. Boyle rolled forward, gaining altitude and greatly enjoying the flight. Then he looked down at the ground again. He was not on his way to Philadelphia. He had learned the terrain from Washington to that city. He had memorized it because there were no adequate maps, no radio, or other devices which could help him. Just the knowledge of the way the ground looked from the air would get him to his destination and he couldn't recognize anything. He was hopelessly lost.

There was nothing to do but land, which he did in what turned out to be a small town in Maryland. The ground was not so smooth as anticipated. His landing approach failed and he ended with a broken propeller blade and his one wing destroyed. By the time the embarrassed officer could alert anyone to what happened, it was too late to meet the three hour planned schedule. The following day, after having transferred 7,000 letters to a new Jenny, Lt. James Edgerton flew to Philadelphia. Lt. Boyle was not given a second chance.

While all the confusion was taking place, a slightly less ceremonial flight was inaugurated from New York to Philadelphia. This was made by a Captain Webb, who traveled without incident.

Fortunately for Lt. Boyle, he did not have to accept all the ridicule for failing with his flight. On September 5, 1918, a New York to Chicago air service was launched from Belmont Park. Max Miller, the pilot of one of the planes, encountered bad weather and was forced to land in Danville, Pennsylvania, where he waited out the storm, then got directions to Lock Haven, the second phase of his flight. There was no problem in Lock Haven, though once in the air, on his way to Cleveland, the pilot noticed that the radiator was leaking. He decided to land in an open field and seek water for his plane.

Air travel was almost unknown in 1918 and the farmer who rushed to meet Miller was both frightened and angry about the plane in his field. He aimed his gun at the pilot and wanted to hear none of the excuses. Crops could be damaged, livestock frightened and all for the sake of some worthless machine that fell out of the sky. Miller had to return to the plane and get it out of there or both he and the craft would likely be filled with holes. Empty radiator or not, Miller took off, landing just far enough away to be certain the farmer could not see or reach the *Jenny*.

The repair was made and Miller flew to Cleveland. Then it was on to Chicago without further incident.

The cost of this new air service was fixed at 24 cents for up to one ounce, with stamps in denominations of 6 cents, 16 cents, and 24 cents. There was little demand at first, but the improvements in airplanes, facilities for fueling, and servicing the aircraft, and an effort to increase the distances traveled resulted in cross-continent service of 24 hours in 1921. The planes were flying at night, and at least three days were saved over the delivery of railroad. Businesses were able to save time so the relatively high cost no longer seemed such a major obstacle.

Other countries began issuing regular air mail stamps. Austria started with overprints in 1918, using the word *"Flugpost"* on postage stamps affixed to letters for the Vienna-to-Kiev service. A special "Air Post" cancellation was used on the stamp affixed to a cover for the personal collection of England's King George V, an avid collector. This cover was flown from St. John's, Newfoundland, to Clifden, Ireland, on a 16-hour, 12-minute flight on June 14–June 15, 1919. The use of overprints quickly changed to special air stamps for most of the countries of the world.

Air mail was a service in more ways than speed. Countries with extremely rough terrain found that they could unite their people with air mail instead of the previously essential hand-carrying or slow use of animals. This was a time when roads were limited, cars were relatively few in number, and travel was often as primitive in areas such as South and Central America as it had been for Americans in the early nineteenth century.

There were other unusual experiments with flight during this period. In 1927, ships carrying airplanes began using what is called catapult mail. When the ship was within such a distance from shore that a plane could be launched from the deck and have adequate fuel to reach a landing strip, it would carry the mail to the country. This could speed delivery time by a day or more.

Experiments were also made in sending mail by rocket. Mail was placed in cylinders, then shot by rockets. It went quickly and relatively cheaply. Unfortunately, it was inaccurate at best. It often burned up or went off course and was lost. The more sophisticated rocketry became, the less practical the idea seemed. Regular jet aircraft are almost as fast, far more accurate, and can be used on a routine schedule.

Mail has been carried into space, but only as a curiosity. In 1969, this was done for both fun and profit. The *Apollo 11* crew took a letter to the moon, made a special stamp on the lunar surface, and franked the envelope. The steel die used for the moon stamp was returned to earth and used in the production of 10-cent stamps commemorating the flight. The stamps were readily available (Scott #C76) and are not of great value but certainly have fascinating historical background.

The profit motive was primary when *Apollo 15* went to the moon. The astronauts were given permission to carry certain personal items as souvenirs. Astronaut Al Worden took 100 specially prepared covers. These were to be used both as souvenirs and for profit. However, the public outcry against this attempt to cash in on their flight was so great that NASA confiscated 70 of the covers. Unfortunately, in the meantime somewhere between 500 and 2,000 duplicates were made using the same readily available postage stamps. They are identical in appearance and not even Worden can tell the difference. An additional 100 covers, made by a German stamp dealer and signed by the astronauts, were produced and sold. These are quite different from the original flown covers and are considered valuable. At this writing, there are no known counterfeits of the German creations, which were done with financial benefits going to the astronauts.

Today most countries have stopped issuing air mail stamps for domestic use. Most mail travels by air, and all first-class mail is moved across the United States as quickly as air mail once traveled. Many countries have overseas air mail postage and others simply allow the normal first-class stamps, in adequate quantity, to be used.

The result of this change is that it is possible to collect an entire country's air mail issues, often at relatively little cost. When you add crash covers, souvenirs with special cachets and other related items, you can enjoy a lifetime of collecting with just this one specialty.

UNITED NATIONS

United Nations stamps are meant for postage originating from United Nations' centers, such as New York and Geneva, Switzerland. They can be used to send letters and packages from the UN to most corners of the world, although they must be used at the UN and not the country in which the buildings are located. Thus you can mail a letter from UN Headquarters in Manhattan to Brooklyn with a UN stamp, but if you walk a few blocks to a Manhattan post office and try to mail that same letter to Brooklyn, you will have to buy a United States stamp as well.

United Nations stamps have always been designed to make money for the United Nations. There is no reason for a separate postal system from that of the host country, other than the fact that there can be a profit from the sale of commemoratives. However, the fact that these are stamps from a world organization meant to try and bring peace and unity among all nations makes them popular with even most "purists" in philately.

The first United Nations stamps were issued in 1951 with the 1-cent magenta "Peoples of the World" issue. That same year, the various denominations showed the Headquarters' building, the symbol of the United Nations Children's Fund, and other functions of the UN. Most of the stamps during the first ten years reflected UN activities, with a gradual change to commemoratives relating to events of world concern, such as weather, atomic energy, refugees, the economic development of underdeveloped countries, and the like.

Most of the United Nations issues are representational rather than the specific artwork found with the stamps of most countries. This modern art concept also reduces the chance of problems with member nations. There are countries where religious beliefs among many of the people prevent the human image from being shown in detail in drawings, on coins, and in any similar manner. Most relate this "taboo" to the interpretation of the Ten Commandments in the Old Testament of the Bible. The people believe that humans were created in the image of God and so the drawing or engraving of a human face is actually creating an idol and being sinful in the eyes of God. A modern art, representational approach to the stamps helps avoid conflicts with those who hold these beliefs.

Stamps also are available from the UN in Geneva, Switzer-

Someone interested in United Nations stamps might want to join an organization devoted exclusively to their issues as well as a general society such as the American Philatelic Association.

land, and, most recently, from offices in Vienna, Austria. The addresses are found in the Appendix.

THE TALKING STAMPS OF BHUTAN

Stamp collectors have varying ideas as to what is proper and improper in their field. A stamp is meant for postage. It should serve the needs of the mailing public. The "purists" among collectors become irate when a country issues more stamps than it needs for postage just to raise money from collectors who will buy the colorful pieces of paper to save rather than utilize.

However, there can be exceptions when the issues are colorful enough and unique. They will never have investment value and fellow collectors may think you are a little foolish, yet you can have a grand time enjoying your hobby. One such country is Bhutan.

Bhutan is a Himalayan kingdom about the size of Vermont and New Hampshire. Poverty is so great that the per capita income is less than $100, earned from products ranging from cloth to yak butter to elephants. The King, Jigme Singye Wangchuck, born in November 1955, has the responsibility of trying to maintain the health and upgrade the standard of living of his people, whose average life is less than forty-three years.

There has never been much to offer outsiders from Bhutan. The country was originally ruled by Tibet in the sixteenth century, with Britain gradually taking control by the 1900's. The monarchy was established in 1907, the country becoming a British protectorate three years later, then gaining independence in 1949. India currently supplies what little outside aid is available, yet the country is so poor that even the World Bank will not provide loans. There is no way to pay them back.

One of the members of the royal family was educated at Oxford University in England. While there, she befriended an American named Burt Kerr Todd, a fellow student who was fascinated with the woman's story of her native country. He decided to visit Bhutan with some friends after graduation. They journeyed to the capital city of Thimphu and were enamored with what they found.

Todd was an extremely successful executive in the steel industry and became actively involved as a financial adviser to the Bhutan government. His concern was with raising the income level of the country in order to improve the quality of their extremely hard life.

After the turn down of a World Bank loan, a suggestion was made to Todd that he explore the philatelic sales industry. Creating stamps for collectors might be a way for Bhutan to improve its financial picture without great expense.

The result of this suggestion was the most unusual marketing programs ever created. It is a delightful philatelic specialty that perhaps as many collectors love as hate. The stamps have included three-dimensional views of outer space, visible without special glasses; steel industry commemoratives printed on steel foil; talking, musical records telling the story of Bhutan, and numerous other concepts. Some of the stamps are meant to have an appeal to topical collectors, such as issues featuring dogs like the Lhasa Apso, the poodle, and others. Other issues are meant to relate directly to the culture and people of the country.

The issues of Bhutan are ingenious, fascinating, and go far beyond the postal needs of so poor a country. The major stamp collecting organizations, such as the American Philatelic Society and the Royal Philatelic Society, do not consider these stamps to be legitimate issues. However, the true collector does not care. The postal issues are fascinating and they play a legitimate, though mostly nonpostal, role in the country's economic affairs. Thus this can be an area in which you specialize, so long as you recognize that the value of such issues will probably never rise.

OTHER COLLECTIBLES

Anything related to philatelic activity has become a collectible for those interested in the postal services around the world. One popular area is the American duck stamp and related material. The duck stamps are issued annually for hunting licenses. Not only are these collected independently of the licensing use, the artists' renderings used during the creation of each stamp are avidly collected for prices usually starting at several thousand dollars.

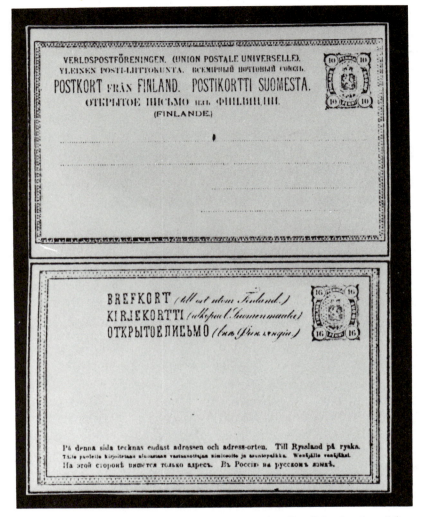

This postcard from Finland is a typical postal collectible that is neither a stamp nor a cover.

Signed lithographs of postage stamp designs are also popular. The United Nations Postal Service released two stamps in 1982 which had been created by actress Sophia Loren. The Italian actress, internationally known for her film work is also an artist and lithographs of her two stamp designs were printed in limited (1,000 copies) editions. These were signed and sold for approximately $75 each in order to raise money for various UN activities. The signed lithographs related to the stamps became as collectible as the stamps themselves.

Some collectors like to obtain covers which have carefully created themes. For example, a growing number of collectors like stamps related to baseball. Although such issues have been quite limited in the past, the number of such issues is expected to grow now that baseball is being planned for the Olympics. The specialized collector will often send a cacheted cover to various team members of World Series championship teams, pennant winners, the players in an All Star game or almost any other professionals. Eventually autographs are obtained on the covers and the collector has a highly personal, created collectible related to a special interest.

The key to philately as a hobby is personal interest. The field is so broad and there are so many ways you can enjoy it without just collecting stamps that literally everyone can find something he or she likes. You are limited only by your imagination in your choice of how you will enjoy your hobby.

10

Investing in Stamps

There is going to come a day when you want to own one or more stamps because you are hoping it will increase in value. You may need the stamp as part of your collection and be inwardly pleased that a high-quality example of that issue has risen steadily over the years. Or you may find a good buy on a stamp that is of investment quality and decide to buy it even though the country or origin, the topical, or some similar aspect is different from your usual interest. Whatever the case, even a beginner needs to understand some of the ramifications of this decision and how to avoid having problems.

Several factors help determine when a postage stamp is of investment caliber. The main ones are availability and demand. Rarity by itself does not effect the value. For example, suppose that there are just a dozen examples of a particular stamp. Since most stamps are printed in quantities ranging from several hundred thousand copies to many millions, a stamp for which twelve examples exist is obviously quite rare. But does this make it valuable?

Suppose there are five collectors who want to own the twelve stamps and that the current owners want to sell them. This means that seven more stamps are in existence than there are buyers for them. Obviously the buyer has the advantage because he or she can bargain down the asking price. After all, if one owner tries to hold out for a high figure, the potential buyer can simply go to a second owner who is more reasonable. This lack of buyer interest means that the stamps will stay quite inexpensive.

On the other hand, suppose there are several hundred stamp collectors who want to own an example of one of those twelve stamps. Each of the potential buyers is willing to bid against the others in order to gain one of the specimens. The prices rise steadily because there is constantly more of a market than there are stamps. Thus DEMAND is as big a factor in determining the value of a stamp as is the rarity.

A third criterion must be considered when thinking of value. If you are interested in investment, you are not thinking of selling your stamps next week. You might be holding the stamps for retirement or for a "rainy day." Many collectors buy rarities when they can afford them, but concentrate primarily on their general collection. They know that if they ever get into a financial bind, they can sell one or more of the rarities to raise money. Then they will have the rest of their collection to enjoy. This means that the investment stamps must be in demand, not only now but in the years ahead. For this reason, most stamp experts suggest avoiding recent issues because they have not proven their sustaining power.

Every year many countries of the world produce stamps on a particular theme and sell them to collectors. Often the theme relates to such popular topics as Britain's Royal Family or international athletic events. Countries issue stamps and many dealers offer the opportunity to buy all issues.

Some of the issuing countries try to create instant "rarities" by limiting the number of souvenir sheets, high-value stamps, or some other aspect of their issues. Thus they have common stamps available plus some that cost several dollars when issued. They often release fewer of these "scarce" items than they know demand for the more common stamps is likely to be. This result is that certain items, upon being issued, command a high price. Then, during the course of the year, there is a fairly brisk resale market that also drives prices higher.

Finally, the event being commemorated is over. Everyone who wanted the series has all or most of the stamps and souvenir sheets issued. The albums are put away for a few years while the owners get interested in other stamps. Then, at some point, many sell their "investment."

At the point of resale a few years after the Silver Wedding Anniversary or a particular Olympic games or the wedding of Prince Charles, or whatever, reality comes into play. Often the "scarce" stamps and souvenir sheets that created a mild stir when issued are no longer in demand. They may even have been issued by countries that are not popular with collectors. The people who truly wanted the stamps own them and there is no resale market.

True rarities have such few stamps available that the prices always go up. Once stamps cost several thousand dollars each, there is no way to manipulate the market easily. Only a millionaire could buy everything, then control the release to effect the prices and this has not happened. However, scarce stamps have been manipulated and the *Graf Zeppelins* are a good example of what can occur.

There are many types of investment purchases because investments, unlike stamps purchased for pleasure, can be anything. You can delight in collecting the stamps of Poland because many of the more recent issues are magnificent art reproductions and other popular topicals. Yet when you decide to buy for investment, you might select a rare air mail stamp from the United States, even though your regular interest is not air mail. You choose the investment item for its resale history, not necessarily because it fits into your collecting interest. Consider the following when evaluating a stamp for investment.

How well has the stamp done in the marketplace over the years? Many dealers feel that material fifty years old and older is the best investment area, no matter how good some more recent issues may prove. A fifty-year track record provides adequate indication of what the future is likely to be.

What kind of appeal do the stamps have? Rare stamps always have the greatest market in the country of origin. If you live in the United States, you will have the broadest resale potential with U.S. rarities. The same is true if you live in England, Canada, Australia, or anywhere else. But many stamps also have international appeal and make good investments.

The stamps of England are always popular with collectors because of their historic importance. England was the home of the first widely used postage stamp and most investors are aware of the country's popularity. In fact, during the 1970's, many Arab leaders recognizing that their oil reserves were quite finite, invested in rare postage stamps. These purchases included the great rarities of England because of their popularity internationally.

Other countries whose stamps are internationally popular are the Vatican, Israel, and Ireland. Irish stamps draw less attention than stamps of the Vatican and Israel because they lack the religious connection which generates popularity for them. However, the Irish have a romance about them that seems to be interna-

tionally infectious. Irish stamps can be sold to dealers in France or Japan almost as easily as to dealers in the United States and England.

The stamps of the country in which you live are still the best for long-term investment. However, the countries named all have universal appeal, with Canada and Australia rising in popularity among both British and American collectors.

SPECIFIC TYPES OF STAMPS

Topical stamp collecting is a growing area of popularity. You might buy stamps featuring sports or cars or almost anything else. And among the topicals are air mail stamps, which have strong investment value among some issues.

Air Mail

In the United States, the Zeppelin stamps of 1930 are the best known air mail investments. These are the *Graf Zeppelin* (blimp) issues in denominations of 65 cents, $1.30, and $2.60, which are listed as Scott U.S. C13 through C15.

Air mail stamps of many other countries have similar items within their history. The early air mail stamps were usually postal tools rather than collectibles. Thus most were used and the number available is often small.

United Nations

Collectors were slow to be interested in the United Nations. The early stamps did not sell particularly well and remain relatively low-priced despite a growing number of specialists.

In 1955, the United Nations produced a souvenir sheet (Scott #38) which contains reproductions of the 3-cent, 4-cent, and 8-cent stamps for that year. The quantities were fairly limited because interest was low. There were two printings, the first one having a broken line of background shading on the 8-cent stamp. A small white spot is visible below the left part of the *"n"* in *"Unies."* This was retouched before the second printing.

Not long after the issue of the souvenir sheet, the United Nations decided to begin promoting its postal issues. They put together a portable display unit in a mobile van. The van traveled throughout Europe, introducing thousands of collectors to the potential of the United Nations issues.

The result of the promotion was that a growing number of collectors began buying United Nations stamps. The issues in recent years have had extremely large printings and the early year issues have risen steadily. However, the major investment benefit has been with those who purchased the souvenir sheet of 1955.

The United Nations stamps form a series which almost every collector can either afford to own or can anticipate buying in its entirety. The price of the early souvenir sheet is still low enough that its purchase seems realistic and it is currently the only item which is truly high priced.

Australia and Canada

Australia and Canada have had limited numbers of stamps issued during their early years. Australian stamps date to 1913 when the country was still sparsely populated. The Canadian stamps date to 1851, again at a time when the stamps met the needs of the people and the population was limited. Thus the demand for these stamps is far stronger than the available issues, a fact guaranteed to keep the issues rising steadily.

STAMP SPECULATION

In the early 1970's, it was possible to buy the C13 through C15 issues for approximately $1,500 to $2,000 in mint, never hinged, superb condition. There would be full margins, the gum would be perfect, and the stamps would be the best of the printer's art for that period. This was also a price affordable for a number of individuals who decided to try and corner the market. Thousands of dollars were spent by these individuals so that they could own several sets in the best possible condition. Sometimes these were the superb stamps, other times they were of lesser quality. But quantity purchases were made either way, steadily raising the price to between $8,000 and $10,000. The wholesale price rise to approximately $6,000 or a 400 percent average return between the retail purchase and the wholesale resale for the early speculators who pulled out after holding their stamps less than five years.

By the end of 1981, the market plummeted. Auction sales were in the $2,000 to $2,500 range for the same stamps. Not only were the stamps being dumped, new buyers were afraid to bid very high for fear there would be another drop in the market.

The following year the prices began to stabilize at a slightly higher figure, though still half or slightly less than what they were at the peak of the speculation. The stamps remain good investments. They will rise steadily in the years ahead. However, the period of speculation has rightfully frightened many would-be investors.

The only safe way to buy investment-quality stamps, beyond following the age rule mentioned, is to observe the market carefully. Stamps of investment quality have legitimately risen 15 to 20 percent a year on the average and sometimes more. This has occurred during recessions, depressions, and periods of strong economy. All anyone interested in investment has to do is take a look at the price changes in annual catalogs such as the Scott or Minkus lines. If your local library does not have them, for a small fee you can join the American Philatelic Society and utilize its library to do your research. The catalogs are loaned by mail for the price of the postage if you are a member.

Generally it is wise to avoid speculated issues. If you are not certain which issues are speculated, use a 25 percent maximum annual rise as a guide. Once stamps start exceeding such an increase in price, you can be fairly certain speculators are involved. A very rapid gain in a short period of time means that you should wait to buy until the supplies are unloaded and the market price drops. Then buy at the first hint of a turn-around after the price stabilizes and starts a normal growth. You are always better off buying stamps at perhaps 10 percent more than their bottom price than you are buying when they are at peak of speculation or even rapidly rising. Slow and steady growth is the key to long-term investment-grade material.

THE PROBLEM OF COUNTERFEITS

Any time you have valuable art objects that are fairly easy to reproduce, you are also going to have counterfeiters. The makers of false stamps are often legendary. Some have been more skillful than the original painters. During the American Civil War, manufacturers of counterfeit Confederate postage stamps and currency often produced work more acceptable to the citizens of the Confederacy than their own government's issues. They were better made, so it was assumed that they were "real."

One of the finest counterfeiters of the twentieth century was Juan de Sperati. He came from a family of Italians operating out of both Pisa and France. Many of the family members were counterfeiters, but Juan was the best. He obtained the same paper used for genuine stamps, then took great care to match ink, color, and other details. At times he would simply alter an original stamp from a common issue to a rarity, his retouching so skillful that it was almost impossible to tell that his design was printed over the cancellation mark.

Sperati was sought by Edmond Locard, among other members of the law enforcement profession, and Locard was an expert at spotting forgeries. Even he was fooled by some of the Belgium, Hong Kong, and Spanish counterfeits made by Sperati. He considered several of the forged stamps to be genuine, a fact the forger corrected during his trial.

Eventually the British Philatelic Association bought Sperati's stock of stamps in 1953 for ten million francs. They wanted to be certain that no new forgeries would enter the market. Sperati was seventy at the time and agreed to not produce any more stamps for the market. He died four years later, wealthy from his fakes.

Some of the early forgers had stamps so well made that the only difference between theirs and the genuine issues was the quality of the ink. The real stamps were made from ink which faded when the stamp was wet. The forgeries used ink which was color-fast. The only easy test was to dip the stamp in water. Unfortunately, genuine issues were destroyed.

Today the problem of stamp forgeries remains. The various organizations for collectors have studied the problem for many years and a number of authentication services have been developed. You can have your stamps sent to one of these services, such as the one run by the American Philatelic Society (details and addresses are in the back of this book), and they will give their opinion. They may not be perfectly accurate but they are seldom fooled and their decision is usually accepted by all dealers. Naturally the cost, though low, is still high enough that using them is only practical for investment-quality issues.

There are also "Cinderella" stamps on the market. You may run across postage stamps that have never been issued by a country. You can not find them in any of the catalogs and an unscrupulous seller tries to convince you that you have found a rare variety. In reality, you probably have a created issue. These fantasy stamps, often beautifully designed, are called "Cinderellas." They are popular with forgers because their creation does not cause severe problems with the countries involved. Most postal laws are only meant to prosecute the counterfeiters of genuine postage stamps. Creators of issues that have never truly existed easily slip past the law while costing collectors considerable sums of money.

FACTORS IN STAMP INVESTMENT

Once you are interested in investing, subtle differences in printing become important. Color differences can indicate either errors on the stamps or different printings. The C38 United Nations souvenir sheet is an example. The second printing is actually better than the first. It was also printed in a smaller quantity and some collectors are willing to pay slightly more money for the difference.

Color and printing variations appear on numerous stamps over the years. Sometimes there are perforation differences or no perforations when they should exist. There can be watermark variations and numerous other subtle alterations in a stamp effecting its desirability among collectors.

The Glossary provides much of the information you need to understand the various terms you will encounter as you collect stamps. Among the terms to check for investment interest are: "Cinderellas," Blind Perforations, Black Jack, Bull's Eyes, Crash Cover, Perforation, Phantoms, Printer's Waste, Proofs, Replicas, Reprints, and Specimens.

AUCTIONS

There is an excitement to buying at auction. Before the auction, you will have a chance to examine both relatively common stamps and some of the great rarities of philatelic history. A stamp which might exist in quantities as small as four or five examples could be

Rarities such as the One Penny Mauritius may only become available at auction. This is because auctions frequently attract a large group of individuals, many of whom have large sums of money to spend.

sold for six figures and your only chance to view it outside a museum may be at the auction. In addition, you may see some of the most prominent dealers and wealthiest collectors in the world should the auction reflect major holdings. However, no matter how enjoyable an auction may be, it is important that you understand the proper way to use one should you choose to buy there.

AUCTION FEVER

Auction Fever is a disease which affects otherwise rational collectors. They become intrigued with the competition of the bidding and lose sight of the cost of the stamps being offered. An item worth $100 might eventually sell for double that amount because the collector became "hooked" on the idea of "winning." He or she was so determined to outbid other collectors that the fact that the same stamp could be purchased for less from almost any area dealer never mattered. The collector had to "beat" the competition, never thinking that the price being paid was a waste of money.

The cure for auction fever is to recognize that the auction is not the "real world." The atmosphere of competition is encouraged because it does result in higher than retail prices for many items. This is why people sell their stamps at auction. They are not seeking just the fair market value but as much money beyond that as they can get. Such bonuses occur from auction fever with enough consistency that auctions are often the preferred way for marketing.

To avoid the "disease," simply plan for the auction in advance. All auctions have catalogs or some similar method for notifying potential bidders in advance of what will be sold. Study the items, check with dealers to see the prices of the ones you want, then plan your bidding so you never offer more than normal retail.

TYPES OF AUCTIONS

Auctions are of two main types—mail-bid and a combination of mail-bid and in-person sales. Few auctions are mail-bid alone since prices usually rise when you can have people competing with each other in public. The companies that specialize in mail bids usually are offering less-expensive items.

Junior Auctions

Many clubs and conventions run junior auctions for enthusiasts under eighteen years of age. The prices charged for the stamps being sold are fixed so that no one may pay more than a set amount—often $5—for any single lot. Most of the stamps will be worth a few cents apiece at the most so that even competitive bidding stops before you have spent much money. Dealers or collectors supporting junior auction activities may also "salt" the lots so that more valuable stamps are included in packets offered for sale or even are available through single lots. When this occurs, you may be able to buy a stamp worth several times the maximum allowed bid. Such junior auctions teach you how to bid and how to avoid becoming being "taken" by your desire to "win"!

Mail-Bidding

You receive a catalog by mail or read about the auction in the auction dealer's advertising in one of the stamp-collecting publications. The items are listed, a description of their conditions will be provided and, usually, at least some of the items will be photographed so you can loosely compare the description with the item pictured. You mail your bid for the items desired and the highest bid wins.

A mail-bid auction or one in which you mail in your bid will require you to guess how the bidding will proceed. Usually you place a dollar amount on each lot you desire (never bid on more lots than you can afford or you may find yourself winning every bid and then unable to pay). The highest bid wins, though most dealers will only charge a percentage higher than the next highest bid if the difference is great. This is a built-in precaution to safeguard the buyer.

For example, suppose a stamp has a retail value of $500 and you have seen a similar issue for sale at that price in the window of a neighborhood dealer. You decide that you will bid 85 percent of the retail to see if you can get it for a price you know will be higher than dealers will pay. You know that some collectors will go to 90 percent of the retail value or higher but your budget will only allow the lower bid—$425.

The day of the auction arrives and, for some reason, nothing works well on that particular lot. The buyers, with the exception of yourself, are not interested in the stamp. The bids reach the $200 level and stay there. Then the mail bids are compared and someone else has made a high bid for the stamp besides yourself. Her bid is $300, a sum $125 less than what you are prepared to pay. You are the winner and your offer is $75 less than the retail.

Some auction houses will simply send you your stamp for the amount bid. Others will only add a percentage figure—usually 5 percent—above the next highest bid. This is a courtesy to the buyer, so that your actual cost for the items becomes $300 plus 5 percent or $315, a sum $110 less than you had expected, based on your actual bid.

The arrangement for competing bids by mail is always outlined in the catalog of a legitimate auction house. Rules that are standard will be carefully printed. Verbal agreements when you call or talk to the staff mean nothing. Read the fine print as it can save you considerable money.

Live Auctions

Before attempting to buy at auctions, analyze your personality traits. Some individuals are so competitive that they will lose sight of practicality when making their bids. They may start with a top bid in mind, then have someone bid slightly more. In order to top that bid, they will have to spend slightly more than they thought best, but the difference is so little that they figure, Why not? Then that bid is topped, again only by a small amount. They make a new bid, quickly losing sight of the fact that the raises they are making will result in an actual purchase price far higher than intended.

Other individuals may want to win but are willing to sublimate their feelings for the practical side of the marketplace. They set a bidding limit and do not deviate from that amount, even when they will have to up their limit a small amount in order to counter a higher offer. These individuals can buy at auction without overpaying because they have the self-discipline to effectively suppress their competitive urges.

You have an advantage over a dealer at an auction that can help you set your bidding limit. A dealer has to plan for overhead as well as profit. Thus every time a dealer buys a stamp, he or she has to plan on adding at least 20 percent to the selling price. This means that a dealer bidding on the stamps you want will have to bid only to a level where the winning bid, plus 20 percent for personal overhead and profit, does not exceed the price at which other dealers are selling the same item. If the new price does exceed that of others, then the dealer will not be competitive and customers will go elsewhere. As a result, you can bid to within 10 percent of the normal retail selling price as listed in the various advertisements and know that you are buying at a price the dealers can not match.

The Auction House's Markup

Auctions are not in business for your convenience. They all take a percentage for their services and the way in which they take that percentage—usually 20 percent—will determine who pays and how much they pay.

There was a time when the fee arrangements were known as the European and American plans. The European plan charged 10 percent of the winning bid to the seller and 10 percent to the

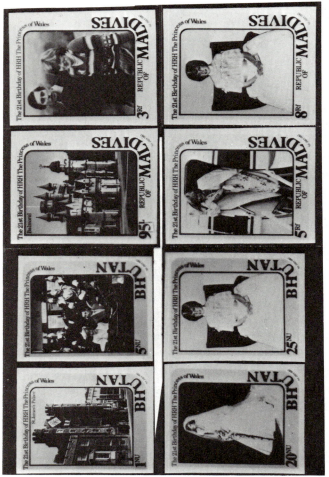

Widely publicized collections of topical stamps such as these related to the marriage of Prince Charles and Lady Diana frequently will appear at an auction. However, complete sets, which may have cost $200 to $300 when new, are seldom desirable for purchase at auction, because usually they will be overpriced by the time a sale is made. Because interest in current topicals wanes after the year of issue, buying these stamps from private collectors who advertise in places like *Linn's Stamp Weekly* is a better way to make this sort of purchase.

buyer. The American plan charged a flat 20 percent to the seller, the fee in all cases based on the winning bid.

For example, suppose your $315 winning bid had been made with an auction house following what was once the American plan. You would pay $315 and be content. The auction house would take your money, subtract 20 percent of that figure ($63) as its commission, then pay the seller $252.

The alternative plan would be to charge both the buyer and the seller a 10 percent fee. This means that you would have paid $315, then been assessed an additional $31.50 as payment to the auction house. Your total payment would have been $346.50. The charge to the seller would be based on your bid, not your final payment. This means that the auction house would pay the seller $315 minus 10 percent of that figure or $285.50. In this second instance, the seller does better than before.

There is no reason to say that one plan is "fair" and another plan is "unfair." Each serves the purpose of moving the merchandise. What is important for you to remember is that if you will pay a 10 percent buyer's commission, you must figure your maximum bid so that the total payment you might have to make is less than the retail price. In our example, the $425 bid, if it won, would have meant a possible payment of $467.50. This was still less than the $500 for which the stamp would have been purchased in a retail stamp shop, so the bid was still fair. Besides, the dealers bidding on the item would have the same fee assessed. Just be certain you understand what you are encountering.

The Careful Approach to Auctions

By spending some time preparing for an auction, you can save yourself costly mistakes.

• Learn something about the company. How long has it been in business? Does it belong to the various dealer and philatelic associations (see Chapter 2)? Does it have a good local reputation? Contact the Better Business Bureau in the city where the company is headquartered for an answer to the latter. All businesses are likely to have complaints against them if they have been in operation a few years, but how were the complaints handled? A satisfactory record in this regard is what you want to check and most BBB offices can help you. Avoid bidding with new auction houses unless they are part of a well-established dealership which is now entering the auction field.

• Study and understand the rules of the auction, which should be explicitly spelled out. Examine the stamps before the bidding.

• Carefully study the dealer's policy on returns. Some dealers feel that return privileges should be stricter for those attending auctions in person than for those bidding through the mail, since the former have the opportunity to examine the stamps before the bidding begins. Unsatisfactory reasons for returning stamps or trying to would be that you decided you could no longer afford the stamps or that you found the same items for less money. There is always a time limit for checking and returning your purchase. Be certain to stick to it. If the time limit is unrealistic, do not bid.

• Make sure you get the stamps described in the catalog or that you examined, and make sure you examine possible purchases carefully before bidding on them. Things like a heavy postmark, thin spots in the paper, and defective gum can easily be spotted. You should have some recourse for improperly or incompletely labeled material, but again, your argument may be weak if it turns out that you bid on a stamp you examined. However, you should be able to get a refund if a stamp turns out to be counterfeit or altered.

• Will the auction house authenticate a stamp for you? Is there time for you to have your stamp or stamps expertized by an organization such as the American Philatelic Society? Although many experienced collectors bidding at auctions run by established houses don't bother with such procedures, you might find this kind of service useful.

• Find out the true market price for every item on which you are bidding. This means more than going to the catalogs. Look in the advertisements in the various journals related to stamp collecting. Most stamps that you will be able to afford are available through dealers so learn their retail prices.

• Never bid more for an item than you will spend buying in a shop. There is no extra value assigned to a stamp because it was sold at auction or came from some well-known collector's estate. The auction house may try to claim that a stamp from a special collection somehow has great historic importance, but in reality an auction is just another type of sale.

11

Clubs, Organizations, and Publications

The beginning stamp collector is always ahead when joining a club, whether local or just becoming a member of a national organization. Groups such as the American Philatelic Society have extensive libraries and other resources available at little or no charge to members. Local clubs offer new friends with shared interests. In addition, you can obtain numerous books and magazines to help your learning.

One of the first things to do as a new collector is to join the American Philatelic Society. You need not do this immediately. In fact, you may find that the monthly magazine produced by the APS is of more detail than you need or want.

A time will come when you want to do more than enjoy the beauty of the stamps and be familiar with the general catalogs. You will want information about history, technical aspects, and similar items. At that time, the American Philatelic Society will handle all your wishes. It not only has over 50,000 members but also has its own large library that will send books to members who want to use them. There are numerous other services, information about which is available by contacting the APS at Box 800, State College, Pennsylvania 16801.

The Society of Philatelic Americans, located by writing to Box 904, Wilmington, Delaware 19809, is quite similar to the APS. There was a time when it was felt that the American Philatelic Society was basically for collectors living in the Pennsylvania area and that the SPA could be more of a Southern alternative. With the ease of transportation, quality of the mail service, and low cost of sending books, magazines and other items to members, the situation has changed. Most collectors belong to one of the two organizations. You will probably want to compare their facilities and services in light of your own personal needs and interests. Then join whichever seems best for you.

The most sophisticated organization for primarily advanced collectors is the Collectors' Club located in New York. This organization has a magnificent old brownstone at 22 East 35th Street, New York, New York 10016. It publishes a technical journal, has meetings twice a month in the city, and actively seeks members throughout the world. This technical organization, whose members are interested in the science and history of philately, is not recommended for the beginner. However, once you have a particular interest and area of specialization (Yes, this might mean the world; some of the Collector's Club members "specialize" in the world), you might want to join both the Collectors' Club and either the APS or the SPA.

Should your interest involve specifically topical categories of stamps, there is a club for you. This is the American Topical Association, 3306 N. 50th Street, Milwaukee, Wisconsin 53216. If you like stamps relating to a particular topic—art, outer space, dogs on stamps, etc.—you might want to join this group. The members try to have programs and writing similar to the APS and the SPA, but with topical emphasis. Again, this is frequently an organization you join at the same time that you become a member of one of the others. It is also fun for the beginner who likes topicals since much of the information will not be too technical.

STAMP CLUBS

Membership in the APS or the SPA is a way of being part of a nationwide organization that holds annual conventions, educational programs, has a library, museum, and other benefits. However, unless you live near the headquarters, your involvement will be primarily by mail. This is often ideal, especially if you are extremely busy and enjoy stamps only in those few free moments you can snatch from your busy day. If you are the type who can spare a few hours a month and wants the companionship of other collectors, then you may also want to join or, when necessary, start a local club.

Existing clubs in your area can be found through one of three sources. Usually your local stamp dealers will know the clubs that exist near where you live. You will also find that your community's Chamber of Commerce may know since most such organizations try to keep track of collector clubs in order to provide such information to new area residents. Finally, you can contact the APS, since they maintain lists of clubs around the country that are affiliates of the APS. Not all clubs have chosen to go this route, but there are so many special programs and advantages for affiliate clubs that many join. The one near you may have this status.

But suppose there is no club near you, or that you find you live in such a large community that the only club is too far from home. Under such circumstances, you might wish to form your own local club.

Basically a club has several purposes, the joy of sharing a hobby of mutual interest being the primary one. You will also want to have presentations on your hobby so that you can gain information beyond what is possible on your own.

Meetings can be held on a rotating basis in the homes of the members. Whoever is not having the meeting in his or her home can provide refreshments. You might also hold your meetings in the public library, since many have free meeting areas for just such organizations. In addition, some savings and loans, banks, and other businesses have meeting rooms available without charge. Just avoid renting space, because you want to keep membership cost to a minimum.

Lectures can be provided by truly knowledgeable collectors willing to share information with the other members. Many stamp dealers can also present programs. If your area dealers are not knowledgeable in special areas, they may still be able to provide basic programs on getting started. In addition, there are programs, including slide shows, available from the American Philatelic Society.

Other possible programs include having representatives from the Post Office discuss the current postal system, available items, and similar information. Your Postal Inspector will be able to provide extremely interesting details on how they operate. The Postal Inspectors have a better record of crime fighting than almost any other law-enforcement agency around the country. History teachers and college professors may be able to provide information on critical periods of postal history—as well as interesting stories about people like Benjamin Franklin, who have influenced the mail system.

The meetings can include a small selling area after the various presentations. Members can sell and trade their stamps among themselves. Area dealers can be invited to participate as well, provided they are also members. While some stamp dealers see their job as selling a commodity, no different from stocks, insurance, or similar items, most thoroughly enjoy the hobby of stamps. They want to share and participate in a local club as a way of doing it. It is a courtesy to include them in the bourse following the meeting.

Large conventions should seldom be attempted by a stamp club. These are usually the realm of either the APS or of federations of clubs within a state, region, or collecting specialty. Such conventions should be outside your concern as a new collector other than to attend them for enjoyment. They require special concerns about security, housing those attending, publicity, and related matters.

Your stamp club can maintain a small library of materials for its members to use. This might include the most recent catalogs of stamp values, such as the Scott or Minkus line, general references on stamps ranging from this book to guides in highly technical areas for the advanced collector, general reference and history books on different countries and their postal service, and various national and international periodicals, such as *Linn's Stamp News, Mekeel's Weekly Stamp News,* and *Stamp World Magazine.* Some books that might be included are *Civil War Patriotic Covers* by G. Walcott, *The U.S. Postage Stamps of the Nineteenth Century* by Lester Brookman, *Postage Stamps and Postal History of Canada* by W. S. Boggs, and *The Encyclopedia of the British Empire* by Robson Lowe. These can be purchased from stamp dealers (since many are out of print) and specialty bookstores, with the members of the club sharing the cost.

There are many ways to maintain a club library. One is to have one person in charge who either brings the materials for members to use an hour or more before and after the regular meetings. Another is to have the librarian be someone who can open a room of his or her home to members on a set schedule so the materials can be used there. Yet a third way is to have all materials donated to the reference division of your local public library in the name of the club. The books are placed in a special section and available for use only within the library. Not only does this help you share your knowledge and love of philately, it also makes someone else responsible for the care of the work. The fact that it is non-circulating also means it will not be lost or damaged in someone's home as can be the case when the work is held by club members or the general public.

The publications obtained can be decided by the club members. Either special assessments should be made to meet the costs, or a portion of the dues should be used to buy the books. You might also have members and dealers donate inexpensive duplicate stamps for sale, the club book fund keeping all the proceeds. Even the least desirable stamp may sell for a cent or two to someone who needs it to fill a hole in the collection, and such small amounts do add up.

Buy books according to a group plan to make a complete library. Avoid special-interest purchases and start with the books of general interest that are more expensive than your members can afford individually. You should try to touch upon most of the major interests in world philately (or related to your topic if a topical club) so that members can branch away from their current collecting special interest. This makes the purchases far more valuable than if left to the taste of the librarian or some other person who may want the library more as a personal reference tool than a guide for everyone.

Here are the names and addresses of some periodicals:

Linn's Stamp News, 911 Vandemark Road, Post Office Box 29, Sidney, Ohio 45367.

Linn's World Stamp Almanac, 911 Vandemark Road, Post Office Box 29, Sidney, Ohio 45367.

Stamp World Magazine, P.O. Box 601, Sidney, Ohio 45365.

Scott Stamp Monthly and *Scott Chronicle of New Issues,* P.O. Box 2005, Mahopac, New York 10541.

Stamp Collector, P.O. Box 10, Albany, Oregon 97321.

Stamps Magazine, 153 Waverly Place, New York, New York 10014.

12

Four Thousand Years of Postal History

In order to fully appreciate your new hobby, you might be interested to learn the various ways the postal system developed. Stamps may be relatively recent as an invention for moving the mail but the ways in which messages were sent over the years forms a fascinating aspect of hobby lore.

The exact starting point of the postal service is unknown. The records of various countries that have survived indicate that it is at least 4,000 years old. Messengers traveled on regular routes in the Indus Valley at that time. The Chow Dynasty of China (1122 B.C. to 255 B.C.) had a well-established service, and Egyptians delivered mail at least as far back as 3000 B.C.

The most common mail delivery involved relays of runners when horses or other animals were not available. The messages might be oral or written, depending upon the literacy of the parties involved and other factors. One of the most famous messengers was the Greek who ran from Marathon to Athens, a distance of slightly more than 26 miles, collapsing and dying after announcing the military victory. Such extreme dedication was not expected, though, and relays were often set up to allow maximum speed for the runners without destroying them in the process.

The Bible is an excellent source of postal information. The Book of Jeremiah, for example, discusses: "One post shall run to meet another, and one messenger to meet another, to show the King of Babylon that his city is taken at one end." (Jeremiah, 51:31). And the Book of Job, considered even older than Jeremiah, makes reference to the post or mail service.

The term "post" as used in the Bible refers to a series of runners or riders carrying messages. The origins of the word in

Latin, Italian, and French all are more closely associated with the placement of the letters at a fixed spot. This means the "posting" of mail at a special building or other location.

"Mail," another common term today, came from the time when messages were considered so valuable that the pouches were made from the interlocking metal rings used to make clothing to protect knights. This chain mail which would help ward off blows from weapons served as a pouch and thus the letters which were protected came to be called "mail."

EARLY STAMPS

The earliest stamps were not meant to indicate prepayment of postage but rather to provide proof of safety and authenticity. For example, a seal, actually a metal or clay design impressed into wax or other soft material, identified the sender. An illiterate person could recognize the different symbols created by the seal. When letters could be folded or encased in a pouch, a wax seal might be impressed over the paper so that this seal had to be broken in order to read the contents. A letter received with the seal unbroken insured the privacy of the message.

SECRECY

The great problem with the early messengers was trying to combine accuracy and secrecy. Oral messages were easily forgotten or confused. Written messages could be read by others, a fact of great concern to the military leaders. Equally of concern was the changing of a written message, since some tablets made of wax or clay could be smoothed, then altered.

The Roman emperors' system of sending letters has resulted in the statement "sincerely," which is commonly part of our normal closing. This evolved from the concern over the chance for changing a message on a wax tablet. A metal tablet, which could not be altered, was called a "*sine cere*" message. This was Latin for "without wax." However, when the term "sincerely" was adopted as our closing, it was meant to indicate to the reader that the letter was an accurate reflection of our feelings.

Another approach to ensuring the confidentiality of a letter was developed by King Cyrus of Persia in 559 B.C. He was known to take a courier, usually illiterate, shave his head and have the message stained into his scalp. Then the courier would be isolated until his hair grew back, at which time he would be sent on his way. Only the recipient knew the truth, and he would have the man's head shaved to reveal the message. Since this was before wigs were in popular demand, such messages could not be very timely.

Government leaders often utilized a notebook with pages which were thin sheets of wood covered with wax thick enough to hold a message. The writer would work the wax, hand it to a courier who would take it to the person who needed to be contacted, then wait while that person read it, smoothed the wax, and wrote his reply.

During times of strife, the couriers were under strict orders to smooth the wax at the first sign that danger was present. Often the messenger was illiterate, so there was no chance the message could be duplicated.

One of the most ingenious secret letters ever written was designed by the Spartans and was actually a long piece of papyrus leaf wrapped around a stick. Sparta's wartime messengers frequently needed to carry reports from one military leader to another. To do this without risk of the enemy learning the message, two identical sticks were made. The length and diameter were perfectly matched and the sticks were named skytales.

The leader in Sparta would have one of these sticks for each commander he needed to contact. A matching stick was given to each commander. No two commanders had the same type of skytale and the headquarters in Sparta might have several different skytales, one for each of the different commanders with whom contact had to be maintained.

Next a long, thin leaf of a papyrus was wrapped around the appropriate skytale in such a way that the rings touched one another. The message was then written in a straight line along the length of the skytale, each line directly below the previous. When the message was complete, the papyrus leaf was unwrapped and the messengers ran it to the appropriate individual. The leaf was then rewrapped around the duplicate skytale so that it exactly matched the way it had been written. When this was completed, the message could be read. A slight difference in the length or diameter of the stick would make the message incomprehensible.

Thus secrecy could be maintained as long as the skytales were kept in the hands of only those men who were supposed to have them. The papyrus leaf was useless without the stick for reading.

The Incas of Peru developed an interesting method for secret-message writing that evolved from an accounting tool. A strap with other straps hanging from it, or a strap, stick, or other device with twine hanging from it had been an accounting device in many countries. Often the straps or twine were of different colors, but knots always were tied in them. Each strap represented a different item, and each knot represented a certain number. Thus one strand might represent horses, another strap gold, another corn, and so forth. A knot or knots in the first strand would tell how many horses were owned. The knotting of the second strand might be an indicator of wealth and the knots in the third would indicate quantities of food. Variations of this counting device covered different items and the government might use such a *quipu,* as it was called in Peru, to keep track of soldiers, horses, and weapons. When large sums had to be recorded, a single knot meant 10, a double knot might mean 100 and a triple knot would mean 1,000.

Eventually it was decided to use knot codes for messages other than recordkeeping. Specialists in knot tying and knot decoding were found in each town to ensure the ability to send and receive secret messages.

THE MESSENGERS

The Egyptians were believed to be the first people to have a uniformed message carrier. The postrunners usually carried spoken messages and were selected for their ability to remember complex messages, word for word. It was a status symbol to be one of these runners and, in the eleventh century, they were provided the insignias meant to enhance this image. They were issued a badge which held together a yellow silk scarf. The scarf was designed to hang around the neck and tie in back. The badge, usually either silver or copper, had the reigning monarch's title on one side and a quotation from the Koran on the other.

The Arab world frequently identified horses used for courier service by having the tails of their horses and mules specially bobbed. In fact, the postal service was known as ''baryd,'' a variation of the Persian word *buryda,* which meant "cut off."

Letter writing was a skill known by few over the centuries. The idea of oral communication was always respected and was a common method not only for sending messages but also for coping with stress. The physically fit among the careful listeners would become part of the postal system. Those who were older or less able often became listeners who were paid to hear whatever information the people who paid them wished to impart. This might range from a man complaining about his failures in love to a statesman admitting his fears about his ability to lead. The listeners would hear them out, asking questions when necessary, but offering no judgment. However, when literacy increased within a country, more written messages were sent.

Often the messengers were connected with guilds, especially during the Middle Ages. Professions had groups of people working together for a common interest and, among them, were those who were literate. The adaptation of the horse to domestic use enabled guilds of the same skills (butchers, for example) to send messengers to different cities to communicate common problems.

POSTAL SERVICES

Many European cities developed mail services as people became increasingly literate. Cities such as Prague and Vienna, where education was prized, maintained a high degree of communication.

The importance of the mail service varied with the country. If the mail service was part of a particular city or guild, it was respected, but it did not command the highest priority with the public. However, in a country like Japan, the earliest mail service was connected with the sacred Emperor and the couriers were seen as being sacred to some degree. The messenger would go forth with a box of letters attached to a pole he carried. A second runner would move just ahead, carrying a lantern on a second pole. This lantern illuminated the way for the messenger but, more important, was a signal to the public to not interfere with the swift travel of messages. The lantern was more a symbol than a necessity, as was seen when special-delivery letters had to be transported faster than normal. Only the swiftest runners carried them on a relay basis. The men with lanterns did not go out because they would have forced the letter carriers to slow their pace.

The postal system considered the most important in the development of our modern practice is credited to the Austrians early in the sixteenth century. Emperor Maximilian I wanted a permanent service to take messages throughout the Empire. However, he did not want to be bothered with the implementation of this necessity and thus he was receptive to the suggestion of Francesco de Tassis of Italy. The family of Tassis had a long history of involvement in communication and writing. Some of the ancestors, such as Torquato, a poet, took the name Tasso. Omodeo Tasso, for example, was known for his creation of the Bergamascan Couriers, who carried mail and oral messages in the thirteenth century.

Francesco de Tassis offered to carry mail between Vienna and the Netherlands. The Emperor would be charged nothing for official messages. However, the Tassis family would have an exclusive right to use the service, both when it was established on January 18, 1505, and into the future.

The earliest Austrian postal route under Tassis linked Vienna and Brussels, since these were the cities of greatest concern to the Emperor. Then the Vienna route was extended into Spain and Italy, while the Brussels route extended into Spain and France. First the major cities of strategic and/or political importance were linked, then the lesser cities were added. Horses were kept in special stables so the carriage teams could be changed at regular intervals.

The Tassis family name was later changed, the heirs calling themselves Thurn and Taxis, depending upon where they lived. The succeeding generations extended their service into Germany and elsewhere, creating links with much of Europe.

Francesco de Tassis, also known as Francis von Taxis, was made a postmaster on March 1, 1500, by Philip I, son of the Emperor. This appears to have been a partial test of Tassis' ability, for there is little record of his actions until five years later. At that time he signed a contract guaranteeing him 12,000 livres for the courier service. In addition to linking the cities mentioned, he also had to set maximum delivery times. These included the Brussels to Innsbruck trip in 6½ days (winter) and a day faster in the summer. Brussels to Paris was to take 44 hours. Brussels to Toledo, Spain, was to take 12 days.

The Emperor found that the cost of the postal system was too great for the royal budget. As a means of keeping it solvent, the

Tassis family was allowed to promote private mail and passenger service, as long as it did not interfere with royal trade.

The Thurn and Taxis service was the most reliable and successful at that time. Most communities welcomed it, though there were some areas where a private postal service already existed. Couriers were occasionally killed in an effort to intimidate the local officials so they would refuse to change the existing service.

During the same period when the Thurn and Taxis family service was spreading throughout Europe, a one-man mail operation was taking place. The Dutch scholar Erasmus, who died in 1536, wrote letters in such quantity that he required his own couriers. Since he was idolized by young scholars, he found he could convince them to carry his messages on horseback several times a year. They would travel to distant lands, then gather return mail, gifts, and other items for them. These student/postmen were called *formuli* and allowed him to communicate on a far grander scale than scholars had previously been able to do.

The letter carriers were constantly attempting to innovate ways to speed the mail. One problem they encountered was violence along the roads when a country was in political turmoil. Not only were roads occasionally damaged or destroyed by passing troops, they were also a good location for robbers. Most postmen felt they were only safe when hand carrying items or when traveling on horseback because of the speed and mobility the animal provided. Stagecoaches pulled by teams of horses were more practical in terms of capacity but also required an armed guard accompanying the coach due to greater vulnerability.

Typical of the criticism was a statement made in Britain's Parliament. The English House of Commons was debating the heavier use of stage travel to move mail in the late 1600's. Roads had been repaired and the country was relatively peaceful. However, the critic, a man who was urban-bred and had no interest in such travel for himself, commented:

"It cannot be healthy for anyone if he has to crawl out of his bed one or two hours before sunrise to board a stage-coach. With the greatest of speed they carry him till late at night from one place to another. And so he sits all day long in the stage-coach, in summer half choked by dust and heat, in winter half frozen and hungry. And finally in torch-light he reaches the public house. The next day they load him again into the stage-coach so early in the morning that he does not even get time to have his breakfast. Is it good for a man's health or his business if he travels with sick people or crying children; if he has to endure all sorts of moods, if he is bothered by stinking smells and crippled by boxes and bales? Is it good for your health when they overturn the stage-coach on bad roads, when you have to wade through mud and sit in the cold and wait till they bring new horses to drag the stage-coach away? Is it good for your health to travel in rotten carriages till the axle breaks, or the wheel? And then one has to wait for three or four hours or for half a day and one has to travel all night to make up for the lost time.''

The criticism may have been richly deserved, but stage-coaches were too practical to be ignored. They also opened communication because the cost of stagecoach travel was so low that even the poor could visit far-off communities. Widespread travel led to less provincialism, more contact between communities, more letter writing, greater curiosity about the wider world all around and, eventually, more stagecoaches. Everything fed on itself, the service growing faster, more efficient, cheaper, and more common to use.

Variations of the stagecoach existed in lands where overland travel was too difficult for wheels. Sleds were used in countries with heavy snow. These were much larger than normal and carried considerable weight. Oxen were used with carts in areas where horses were not available and the bicycle was utilized after its invention.

EARLY STAMPS; MAILBOXES

The two important devices that altered the mail after the postal systems were developed were the postage stamp (originally simply a stamp placed on a message) and the mailbox. The earliest stamps were embossed and are known at least as far back as 1435.

By 1454, we know that an inked stamp was used on mail. Then, in 1680, London, England, established a triangular hand-stamp to indicate that the penny post had been paid. This was used by William Dockwra, who ran the post office in the various districts of the city. Nineteen years earlier, Henry Bishop had used a circular stamp which gave the month and year that it was used.

All of these helped with records and ensured that messages were not sent without payment.

Mailboxes or official letter-drop boxes originally were kept by churches in Florence, Italy, back in the 1500's. However, they were not widely used by other countries until they began to be used in Paris in 1653. Even then they would not have been accepted had it not been for a rather torrid love affair taking place.

The Paris postmaster general was under orders to check all letters at a central collection point. Letters were not to be sent with more than one sheet of paper used. Each letter had to be opened and examined, a fact which quickly led to corruption. The leading politicians, often members of the church, would have censors read the letters to learn what was happening. Anything improper that might be taking place, whether a love affair or political intrigue, could not be set to paper and sent through the mail or it would be discovered.

The Marchioness of Longueville apparently knew about drop boxes and decided that this would be the answer to the problem. The sealed boxes did not stop the censorship, but they did prevent the corrupt postal officials from learning the identities of the senders. The letters could be read, though now the senders could use false names and personal codes without anyone connecting the sender with the recipient of the letter. A man could carry on his love affair and the woman could be involved with many others without anyone being the wiser. And the reason the Marchioness developed this service? She was the mistress of the postmaster general.

THE COMING OF THE POSTAGE STAMP

Stamp collectors always look to Britain as the country whose stamps first became important. However, the idea for a postage stamp is believed to have originated within Austria. The year was 1836 and a Slovenian named L. Kosir, an assistant accountant for the state government office in Ljubljana suggested establishing uniform postal rates and adhesive postage stamps. These changes were unacceptable to the government and the idea was lost.

The early British postal system was not very effective. A

series of post lines and postmasters was established. Private carrying of the mail was forbidden and the public treasury paid the salaries and expenses of the workers. However, ninety-nine postmasters petitioned the Council in 1628 because they had not been paid for the previous seven years and some were going to jail for debts.

Mail was carried on foot more than by horses, yet either way the mail seldom moved faster than 18 miles a day.

The first improvement came with a special system of postal roads. Major cities were linked and then smaller communities became trunk lines. Careful arrangement of foot and horse stations allowed the carriers to move the mail at a rate of 120 miles per day. Thomas Witherings was placed in charge of the system and opened it to all people in 1637. No longer would just those designated by the Crown have the privilege. Thus the public would have better communication and begin sharing the cost of a mail service.

Witherings developed a system of controlled rates for postage, the first to be widely used throughout England. Previously, individual towns had mutual mail agreements concerning items sent, but these varied from community to community. Barnstable to Exeter had one rate charged for handling certain items and this was different from the London to Plymouth expenses.

Witherings' scale was based on a single letter, double letter, and everything larger than a double letter. The larger items were sent by the ounce. Smaller letters were charged according to one or two pages of writing. The minimum rate was 2d for a single letter, 4d for a double, and 6d an ounce for everything larger when the item was sent a distance less than 80 miles. The single- and double-letter rates were doubled for anything traveling 80 to 140 miles, the larger packages going for 50 percent more in fees. An additional 50 percent charge for the single- and double-letter rate was used for items traveling more than 140 miles, though still within England (12d per ounce for larger items). Additional rates handled the England to Scotland and England to Ireland mail.

Service was a primary concern of Witherings because there were numerous private posts in competition. The higher speed service cost less in on-the-road expenses to mail a letter.

By the end of the seventeenth century, letter carriers were found only in London. Other cities had a single postmaster who might personally deliver items or just hold them to be picked up. The salaries were small, and in some instances the postmaster earned nothing. He was expected to live in a home large enough to take in travelers. It was the money from passing lodgers that paid for his services. This was not as bad as it sounds since there would be no competition for transient living space in such communities, but the annual income was still extremely low.

The quality of the service had deteriorated to the point where the average letter moved only 4 miles per hour, the speed of a rapid walk. Many individuals became special carriers, taking a horse and riding as rapidly as possible to deliver even a single letter. The charge was three pence a mile for the special service, a bargain when a letter had to be delivered promptly. There was also a long distance rate of six pence for 12 miles, a distance known as a "stage."

The problems with the postal service were compounded by the fact that newspapers were becoming quite numerous throughout England. People were traveling and seeking information about other communities. These papers had to be mailed and customers wanted to be able to have reasonably timely awareness of the news.

In addition to the problems with speed and delivery, corruption was rampant. Some of the post carriers accepted bribes to deliver the mail. At times, packages were opened and the contents shared. Many of the riders were irresponsible teenagers who often saw no reason not to help robbers interested in the contents of their parcels.

The next major innovation, which gradually began to improve the declining service, was the idea of John Palmer of Bath. He was a businessman of the 1780's who recognized that he could travel from Bath to London faster than he could send a letter between those cities. His means of transportation was the stagecoach, not a private horse, so he thought that if the public coaches could carry the mail, the speed of service would improve.

Logical as it sounds today, the use of stagecoaches to carry mail had never been seriously considered. Mailbags could travel at as fast as 9 miles per hour that way and service would be improved. An armed guard, carrying two guns, each the equivalent of a modern low-powered shotgun (the blunderbuss), would accompany the mail. Pistols would be carried by the driver, and the guard would be specially trained in making repairs for the coach so he could provide practical assistance in addition to "muscle."

The plan was eventually tried on August 2, 1784, and found to be workable. The speed was not so great as anticipated but it was faster than anything in current use.

Each change in service, each device which speeded the handling, was accompanied by a growing awareness of how much better it could be. However, it wasn't until the 1830's that Sir Rowland Hill devised a system that revolutionized mail and started the use of postage stamps.

POSTAGE STAMPS COME TO AMERICA

All of the problems that existed throughout Europe were, if anything, worse in Colonial America. Settlements were constantly developing. The people were isolated from one another. Travel was difficult and the immigrants were regularly traveling to new territory. The various courier services were similar to the postal systems abroad, and this meant that they were slow, inefficient, and often resulted in the loss of valued items.

Each colony attempted to establish its own service, both for government communication and private citizens. In addition, many of the early postmasters, such as in Boston, published their own newspapers. They carried gossip, information on ships scheduled to arrive from England bringing packages and mail, and other details. These papers were so popular that the slang expression "keeping posted" evolved for someone who kept up with the news of the day.

The postmasters' newspapers also had a certain amount of advertising notices. They circulated throughout several surrounding areas so residents of one city could have access to the gossip of neighboring areas.

There are several famous incidents where a newspaper publisher became a postmaster instead of the reverse being true. One was Ben Franklin whose paper, the Philadelphia *Pennsylvania Gazette,* was typical of the scandalous gossip sheets of the day.

The *Pennsylvania Gazette* was not founded by Franklin. Samuel Keimer started the paper in 1728 and Franklin took over the following year. Franklin not only utilized gossip, he also became the first American publisher to use sex and violence to sell the news.

One often-quoted exerpt from the *Gazette* read: "We hear, that on Tuesday last, a certain c---n---table having made an agreement with a neighbouring female, to watch with her that night; she promised to leave a window open for him to come in at; but he going his rounds in the dark, unluckily mistook the window, and got into a room where another woman was in bed, and her husband it seems lying on a couch not far distant. The good Woman perceiving presently by the extra-ordinary fondness of her bedfellow that it could not possibly be her husband, made so much disturbance as to wake the good man; who finding somebody had got into his place without his leave, began to lay about him unmercifully; and 'twas thought, that had not our poor mistaken galant, called out manfully for help (as if he were commanding assistance in the King's Name) and thereby raised the family, he would have stood no more chance for his Life between the wife and husband, then a captive L--- (Louse) between two thumb nails."

But even the most exciting stories couldn't guarantee the total success of a newspaper. It would get read in the Philadelphia area, of course, but getting it any further presented a problem. The only way for it to travel any distance was for it to be carried by the postman from town to town.

Although many postmasters had newspapers, a privately published newspaper might not be permitted to be carried in Franklin's area. He viewed this as being unfair, since the post riders were permitted to carry all manner of goods for their customers at whatever fees they could get. The only restriction was that the delivery of the mail had to take precedence.

The letters saved from the Colonial era attest to the wide variety of items carried by the post rider. These ranged from books and clothing to, in one case, a team of horses. According to the letter that preceded the teams being posted: "If their legs are fit to bring them, I desire they may be sent by the post, unless some safer opportunity present in two or three days."

William Bradford was the Philadelphia postmaster during the years that Ben Franklin was starting his *Gazette.* Bradford published the American *Weekly Mercury,* which first appeared on December 22, 1719. Bradford's post riders were not permitted to carry any newspaper other than the *Mercury* and the publisher utilized the riders as sources of information concerning the various towns through which they passed. He was thus able to state that he was able to provide far broader coverage of the news of the colonies than could be his rivals.

Alexander Spotswood, once the governor of Virginia, had been named postmaster-general for the British Colonies in 1730. He was determined to improve both the service and the economics and made numerous changes in the system. One of the most notable changes made by Spotswood, was the appointment of the young printer, Benjamin Franklin, as Philadelphia postmaster.

Franklin was fascinated with his new position. He sought ways to innovate service and spent six years refining the system. Eventually (1753) Franklin became deputy postmaster general of the Colonies, sharing this post with William Hunter of Virginia. Many editors complained that their papers were much later than necessary, so Franklin developed a form reply to the complaint. His notice stated:

"Whereas the late Severity of the Weather has occasioned an Irregularity of the State between this place and Philadelphia; Publick Notice is hereby given, That an especial Messenger with the Mail for Philadelphia will be despatched from the Office at Ten of the Clock this forenoon, in order to bring the Stage right again." The message was signed by Alexander Colden, acting under authorization of Franklin, who had encouraged the service innovation.

Franklin brought many innovations to his job, including the establishment of international mail in 1755. Franklin also set standard fees for mailing newspapers throughout the Colonies. All newspapers were mailed at a rate varying with the distance they traveled. The frequency of delivery also increased.

There was one unvarying aspect to the speed with which mail could be delivered. This was the number of miles a horse and rider could travel. There were no higher-speed conveyances, so the speed and endurance of horse and rider determined delivery.

Franklin's innovation was to establish shifts for postal workers, so that the men involved with the system were working around the clock. On January 16, 1764, he wrote: "I will not only mention that we hope in the spring to expedity the communication between Boston and New York, and we have already that between New York and Philadelphia by making the mails travel by night as well as by day, which has heretofore not been done in America.''

The financial success of Franklin and the other postmasters-general who served with him was remarkable. A deficit of over 943 pounds existed during the first four years of his administration, while he straightened accounts and reorganized the system. Then the profit picture changed and the years 1758–1762 saw surplus profits of over 1,438 pounds. When the money was forwarded to the British Post Office, a note was made, stating: ''This is the first remittance ever made of this kind.'' It had previously been assumed that the Colonial postal system, though essential, would always be a losing proposition.

The British government was aware of Franklin's political activities and felt that these were not proper for the Colonial postmaster-general. He was fired on January 3, 1774, in a brief letter from Anthony Todd, his superior. The letter stated:

''I have received the command of His Majesty's Postmaster-General to signify to you that they find it necessary to dismiss you from being any longer their deputy for America. You will therefore cause your accounts to be made up as soon as you can conveniently.''

Franklin's forced retirement as postmaster-general was to be short-lived. When the American Revolution began, the Continental Congress re-established the postal system under its own control. The members resolved, on July 26, 1775: ''That a Postmaster-General be appointed for the United Colonies, who shall hold his office at Philadelphia, and shall be allowed a salary of 1,000 dollars per an; for himself, and 340 dollars per an, for a Secretary and Comptroller, with power to appoint such, and so many deputies as to him may seem proper and necessary. . .''

The record ends by stating: ''The Congress then proceeded to the election of a Postmaster-General for one year and until another is appointed by a future, when Benjamin Franklin, Esq., was unanimously chosen.''

Franklin delighted in having his new position and continued with the Postal Service until 1776, when he was sent to France to work with that government on behalf of the colonists. During his service, he created a 24-hour-a-day service to move the mails faster and more profitably than ever before. He established special boats to provide direct mail between the Continental Congress in Philadelphia and the Southern Colonies and back, thus improving the unity of the rebels. Newspapers became legitimate mailing items for everyone with consistent rates, thus speeding information. In fact, the total service he provided made the Colonial mail a profitable, well organized communication service which carried over after the revolution into the efficiencies of the first United States mail.

Postmaster-General John Niles suggested that postage stamps be used in the United States shortly after they were introduced in England. However, it was not until 1845 that Congress decided that this would be practical. They were authorized, though with no provision for actually printing them. That law also provided a range of changes. These were, according to the Act of March 3, 1845:

"For every single letter in manuscript or paper of any kind by or upon which information shall be asked or communicated in writing or by marks or signs conveyed in the mail, for any distance under three hundred miles, five cents; and for any distance over three hundred miles, ten cents; and for a double letter there shall be charged double these rates; and for a treble letter, treble these rates; and for a quadruple letter, quadruple these rates; and every letter or parcel not exceeding half an ounce in weight shall be deemed a single letter, and every additional weight of half ounce, shall be charged with an additional single postage."

Because there was no provision for printing postage stamps, the postmasters in various communities made their own. These might be woodcuts or some other homemade device. Each inked impression could be applied to letters for mailing as proof of payment. Actual postal stamps were made by a few postmasters, such as Robert Morris of New York. These are all quite rare and desired by collectors.

It was not until March 3, 1847, that government postage stamps were finally authorized. On July 1, 1847, the first United States postage stamps were issued, a 5-cent denomination with the image of Benjamin Franklin and a 10-cent denomination featuring George Washington. These may sell for several hundred dollars, today, depending upon condition. At last, postage stamps had come to America and, almost from the start, the hobby of stamp collecting was born.

By 1850, the stamp-issuing countries of the world were organizing internationally to facilitate moving the mail. The German-Austrian Postal Union was founded in 1850 and Postmaster-General of the U.S., Montgomery Blair, proposed in 1862, that the United States join with European nations the following year to work together for standardization of postal rates and mailing regulations. However, it was not until October 1874, when 22 nations met in Berne, Switzerland, at the first Postal Congress that the Universal Postal Union was formed.

Today mail moves from country to country with the ease that it once moved from city to city. International cooperation has improved the mail and brought a wide variety of postage stamps within everyone's reach.

The respect we have for today's postal service is rooted in history. While all of us may have complaints about individual letter carriers, most of us will agree that the men and women who deliver the mail perform a heroic feat regardless of conditions. The motto of this dedication—"Neither snow nor rain nor heat nor gloom of night stays these couriers from the swift completion of their appointed rounds''—has its origins several centuries before the birth of Christ. The original statement was in ancient Greek and written by the early historian Herodotus. He was describing the postal system of King Darius the Great of Persia.

Appendix

The easiest way to obtain stamps is from your neighborhood dealer and from the dealers who advertise in publications such as *Linn's Stamp News*. However, if you are interested in stamps of specific countries, you may want to keep up with new releases by buying them directly from the country's post office department. This is easily done for dozens of countries and is cheaper for new issues than buying from a dealer, who has to mark up the price that you would be paying. But if you just want the new issues for a special event, such as commemoratives of Britain's marriage of Prince Charles and Lady Diana Spencer, a new-issue service is simpler to use.

Direct sales from a country are generally limited to current issues, including souvenir sheets and First Day Covers. Some will have previous issues available in limited quantity, though only items still common. Most require a deposit. Each time you order, the price is deducted from the deposit.

Here are four tips for buying through the mail: Always write the country first, enclosing a self-addressed envelope with International Reply Coupons of appropriate postage for a response; your local post office can help you with the coupons. When the time comes, do not send money until you understand the available services and their costs. Have your bank arrange for conversion into that country's currency.

If you plan to go into stamp collecting in a big way, you might want to get a post office box and have your stamps sent there. It is safer, and your stamps have less chance of getting crunched in a small mailbox or the letter-carrier's pouch.

Following is a partial list of countries offering stamps through the mail to collectors. *Linn's World Stamp Almanac* lists countries selling through the mail and is regularly updated, and listings also appear in many of the stamp magazines. If you cannot find the address of a country, write to the main post office of that country in the capital city.

POSTAL ADMINISTRATIONS

Algeria—Receveur Principal des Postes, Alger R.P., Algeria

Endora, French—Service Philatelique des Postes et Telecommunications, 61–63 rue de Douai, 75436, Paris, France

Endora, Spanish—Dirección General de Correos, Servicio Filatelico International, Madrid 14, Spain

Angola—Centro Filatelico de Angola, Lda, CP, 2688, Luanda, Angola

Anguilla—The Postmaster, Department of Posts, The Valley, Anguilla, West Indies

Antigua—Philatelic Bureau GPO, St. John's, Antigua, West Indies

Argentina—Sección Filatelia Correo, Central, Local 247, 1000 Buenos Aires, Argentina

Ascension—Postmaster, Jamestown, St. Helena, South Atlantic

Australia—Philatelic Bureau, GPO Box 9988, Melbourne, Victoria 3001, Australia

Australian Antartic Territory—Philatelic Bureau, GPO Box 9988, Melbourne, Victoria 3001, Australia

Austria—Oesterreichische Post, Briefmarkenversandstelle, A-1011 Vienna Austria

Azores—Philatelic Office, Av. Casal Ribeiro 28-2, 1096 Bisbon Codex, Portugal

Bahamas—Post Master General, GPO, P. O. Box N8302, Nassau, Bahamas

Bahrain—Philatelic Bureau, Postal Directorate, State of Bahrain, Arabian Gulf

Bangladesh—Senior Postmaster, Philatelic Bureau, GPO, Dacca, Bangladesh

Barbados—Philatelic Bureau, GPO, Bridgetown, Barbados, West Indies

Barbuda—Philatelic Bureau, Barbuda Post Office, Codrington, Barbuda, West Indies (via Antigua)

Belgium—Regie des Postes, Service des Collectionneurs, Division 1.3.0.2., 1000 Brussels, Belgium

Belize—Belize Philatelic Bureau, GPO, Belize City, Belize, Central America

Berlin—Verstandstelle für Postwertuzeichin, Postfach 12 09 50, 1000 Berlin 12, Federal Republic of Germany

Bermuda—Bermuda Philatelic Bureau, GPO, Hamilton, Bermuda

Bhutan—Philatelic Officer, Philatelic Bureau, GPO, Phuntsholing, Bhutan

Bophuthatswana—Philatelic Services and INTERSAPA, GPO, Pretoria 0001, Republic of South Africa

Brazil—Empresa Brasileira de Correos e Telegrafos, ed. Apolo, Scs, Qadra 13, Bl. A, Lote 36, 7° Andar, 70300 Brasilia, DF Brazil

British Virgin Islands—Postmaster, Philatelic Bureau, Road Cap Town, Tortola, British Virgin Islands

Brunei—Postal Services Department, GPO. Bantar Seri Begawan, Brunei

Burma—Myanma Export Import Corporations, Export Division, Philatelic Section, Rangoon, Burma

Burundi—Agence, Philatelqui du Burundi, Boite, Postale 45, Bujumbura, Burundi

Canada—Philatelic Service, Canada Post, Ottawa, Canada K1A 0B5

Cape Verde Islands—Direccao dos Servicoes de Correios e Telecomunicaçoes, Praia, Republica de Capo Verde

Cayman Islands—Post Master General, Philatelic Department, Grand Cayman, Cayman Islands, West Indies

China—Republic—Taiwan—Philatelic Department, Directorate General of Posts, Taipei 106, Taiwan, Republic of China

Christmas Island—Philatelic Bureau, Christmas Islands, India Ocean

Cocos (Keeling) Islands—Philatelic Bureau, Post Office, Cocos (Keeling) Islands, India Ocean

Columbia—Oficina Filatelica, Administración Postal Nacional, Oficine 209, Edificio Murillo Toro Bogotá 1, Columbia

Cook Islands—Philatelic Bureau, Post Office Box 200, Rarotonga, Cook Islands, South Pacific

Costa Rica—Oficina Filatelica de Costa Rica, San José, Costa Rica

Cyprus—Philatelic Branch, GPO, Nicosia, Cyprus

Denmark—Postens Filateli Raadhuspladsen 59, DK-1550 Copenhagen V, Denmark

Dominica—Post Master, Stamp Order Division, GPO, Roseau, Dominica, West Indies

Dominican Republic—Oficina Filatelica, Dirección General de Correos Santo Domingo, Dominican Republic

Egypt—Philatelic Office, Cairo, Cairo Arab Republic of Egypt

El Salvador—Dirección General de Correos, Departamento de Filatelia, Republic of El Salvador, Central America

Ethiopia—Ethiopian Postal Service, Philatelic Section, Post Office Box 1113, Addis Ababa, Ethiopia

Faroe Islands—Frimerkjadeildin, 3800 Torshavn, Faroe Islands

Federal Republic of Germany—Verstandstelle für Postewertzeichen, Postfach 20 00, 6000 Frankfurt 1, Federal Republic of Germany

Fiji—Philatelic Bureau, GPO Box 40, Suva, Fiji

Finland—General Direction of Posts and Telecommunications, Philatelic Section, Dagmarinkatu 14, P.O. Box 654, SF-00101 Helsinki 10, Finland

France—Service Philatelique, 61–63 rue de Douai, 75435 Paris Cedex 09, France

France Polynesia—Receveur Principal des PTT Service, Philatelique, Papeete, Tahiti, France Polynesia

French Southern and Antarctia Territories—Agence Comptable des Timbres Poste d'outremer, 85 Avenue de la Bourdonnais, Paris 75007, France

Gibraltar—Post Office, Philatelic Bureau, Post Office Box 5662, Gibraltar

Great Britain—British Post Office, Philatelic Bureau Lothian House, 124 Lothian Road, Edinburgh EH3 9BB, Scotland

Greece—Greek Post Office, Philatelic Service, 100 Aiolou Street, Athens 131, Greece

Greenland—Gronlands Postvasen, 100 Strandgade, Post Office Box 100, DK-1004, Copenhagen K, Denmark

Grenadines of Saint Vincent—Bureau Manager, Saint Vincent Philatelic Service, GPO, Kingstown, Saint Vincent West Indies

Guatemala—Dirección General de Correos y Telegrafos Departamento Filatelico, Guatemala, Central America

Guernsey—States Philatelic Bureau, Head Post Office, Guernsey, Channel Islands

Guinea—Agence Philatelique, Boite Postale 814, Conakry, Republic of Guinea

Honduras—Departamento Filatelico, Dirección General de Correos, Tegucigalpa, DC, Honduras, Central America

Hong Kong—Philatelic Bureau, GPO, Hong Kong

India—Philatelic Bureau, GPO, Bombay 400001, India

Indonesia—Philatelic Subdivision, State Enterprise Posts and Giro, 34 Jalan Jakarta, Bandung, Indonesia

Iraq—Posts and Savings Administration, Stamp Department, Philatelic Bureau, Baghdad, Republic of Iraq

Ireland—The Controller, Philatelic Bureau, GPO, Dublin 1 Ireland

Isle of Man—Philatelic Bureau, Post Office Box 10M, Douglas, Isle of Man

Israel—Ministry of Communications, Philatelic Services, Tel Aviv-Yafo 61 080, Israel

Italy—Ufficio Principale Filatelico, via Maria dei Fiori, 00100 Rome, Italy

Ivory Coast—Office des Postes et Telecommunications, Direction des Services, Postaux, Service Philatelique, Abidjan, Ivory Coast

Jamaica—Postmaster, Philatelic Bureau, GPO Kingston, Jamaica

Japan—Philatelic Section, GPO Box 888, Tokyo 100–91, Japan

Jersey—The Jersey Post Office, Philatelic Bureau, Post Office Box 304, Jersey, Channel Islands, via Great Britain

Kenya—Philatelic Bureau, Post Office Box 30368, Nairobi, Kenya

Kiribati (Gilbert Islands)—Philatelic Bureau, Box 494, Betio, Tarawa, Kiribati

Republic of Korea—Korean Philatelic Center, Division of Bando Sangsa Company, Ltd, CPO Box 1899, Seoul, Republic of Korea

Kuwait—Director, Post Office Department, Philatelic Bureau, Safat Post Office, Kuwait

Lesotho—Philatelic Bureau, Post Office Box 413, Maseru, Lesotho

Luxembourg—Direction des Postes Office des Timbres, Post Office Box 999, Luxembourg, Grand Duchy of Luxembourg

Madeira—Philatelic Office, Av. Casal Ribeiro 28–2, 1096 Lisbon Codex, Portugal

Malawi—Post Office Philatelic Bureau, Post Office Box 1000, Blatyra, Malawi

Republic of Maldives—Philatelic Bureau, GPO Male Republic of Maldives, Indian Ocean

Malta—Philatelic Bureau, GPO, Auperge d'Italie, Valletta, Malta

Mauritius—Department of Postes and Telegraphs, GPO Port Louis, Mauritius

Mexico—Departamento Filatelico, Edificio de Correos, la Calle de Tacuba Number 1, Mexico 1, D.F. Mexico

Monaco—Office des Émissions de Timbres-Postes, Department de Finances, Principality of Monaco

Montserrat—Montserrat Philatelic Bureau, GPO, Plymouth, Montserrat, West Indies

Morocco—Ministère des P.T.T. Division Postale, Rabat, Morocco

Nauru—Officer-in-Charge, Philatelic Bureau, Republic of Nauru, Central Pacific

Nepal—Officer-in-Charge, Nepal Philatelic Bureau, Cundhara, Kathmandu, Nepal

Netherlands—Netherlands Post Office Philatelic Service, Post Office Box 30051, 9700–RN, Gröningen, Netherlands

Netherlands Antilles—Philatelic Service Office, Postmaster, Willemstad, Curaçao, Netherlands Antilles

New Caledonia Service—Philatelique, Direction Generale, des P.T.T., Noumea, New Caledonia

New Hebrides Condominium—Philatelic Section, Condominium Post Office, Port-Vila, New Hebrides, South Pacific

New Zealand—Post Office, Philatelic Bureau, Private Bag, Wanganui, New Zealand

Nicaragua—Oficina de Control de Especies, Postales y Filatelia, Palacio de los Heroes de la Revolución, Apartado, 325, Managua, D.N. Nicaragua, Central America

Nigeria—Nigerian Philatelic Service, GPO, Tinubu Street, P.M.B. 12647, Lagos, Nigeria

Nieue—Philatelic Bureau, Box 150, Nieue Post Office, Government of Nieue, Alofi, Nieue, South Pacific (via New Zealand)

Norfolk Island—Senior Philatelic Officer, Norfolk Island 2899, South Pacific

Norway—Postdirektoratet, Posteoks, 1181, Sentrum, Oslo 1, Norway

Sultanate of Oman—Philatelic Bureau, Department of Postes, Telegraphs & Telephones, Muscat, Sultanate of Oman

Pakistan—Pakistan Philatelic Bureau, GPO, Karachi, Pakistan

Panama—Dirección General de Correos y Telecommunicaciones Deparamento de Filatelía, Apartado 3421, Panama 1, Panama

Papua New Guinea—Philatelic Bureau, Post Office Box 160, Port Moresby, Papua New Guinea

Pitcairn Islands—Postmaster, Philatelic Bureau, GPO Box 40, Suva, Fiji, South Pacific

Portugal—Philatelic Office, Ave. Casal, Ribeiro 28-2, 1096 Lisbon Codex, Portugal

Qatar—Philatelic Bureau, Department of Postes, Doha, State of Qatar

Romania—ILEXIM, 13 decembrie St. No. 3, Post Office Box 136-137, Bucharest, Romania

Ross Dependencies—Post Office, Philatelic Bureau, Private Bag, Wanganui, New Zealand

Rwanda—Direction Generale des PTT, Kigale, Rwanda

St. Helena—Postmaster, Jamestown, St. Helena, South Atlantic

St. Kitts—Nevis-Anguilla Postmaster General, GPO, Basseterre, St. Kitts, West Indies

St. Lucia—Postmaster, GPO, Castries, St. Lucia, West Indies

St. Pierre and Miquelon, Service Philatelique, 61-63 rue de Douai, 75436, Paris Cedex 09, France

St. Thomas and Prince Islands—Direccao dos Correios e Tele-comunicações Seccao Filatelica, St. Thomas, Democratic Republic of St. Thomas and Prince Islands

St. Vincent—Bureau Manager, St. Vincent, Philatelic Services, GPO, Kingstown, St. Vincent, West Indies

Republic of San Marino—Philatelic Office, 47031 Republic of San Marino

Senegal—Office des Postes, et Telecommunications du Senegal, Bureau Philatelique, Dakar, Senegal

Seychelles—Philatelic Bureau, Post Office Box 60, Victoria, Maag, Seychelles, Indian Ocean

Singapore—Postal Services Department, 8th Floor, World Trade

Centre, Maritime Square, Singapore 0409, Republic of Singapore

Soloman Islands—Philatelic Bureau, GPO, Honiara, Solomon Islands, South Pacific

Democratic Republic of Somali—Philatelic Services, Ministry of Postes and Telecommunications, Mogadishu, Somali Democratic Republic

Republic of South Africa—Philatelic Services, GPO, Pretoria 0001, Republic of South Africa

South-West Africa—Philatelic Services & INTERSAPA, GPO, Pretoria 0001, Republic of South Africa

Spain—Dirección General de Correos, Servicio Filatelico Internacional, Madrid 14, Spain

Three Sri Lanki—Philatelic Bureau, Ceylinco House, Colombo, 1, Three Sri Lanki

Sudan—Philatelic Office, Posts and Telegraphs, Public Corporation, Khartoum, Sudan

Swaziland—Swaziland Stamp Bureau, Department of Postes & Telecommunications, Post Office Box 555, Mbabane, Swaziland

Sweden—PFA, Postens, Frimarksavdelning, S-105 02 Stockholm, Sweden

Switzerland—Philatelic Service, PTT, Parkterrasse 10, CH 303 Bern, Switzerland

Tanzania—Tanzania Postes and Telecommunications, Department of Postes, Stamp Bureau, Post Office Box 2988, Dar-es-Salaam, Tanzania

Thailand—Philatelic Promotion Center, Commercial Division, The Communications Authority of Thailand, Bangkok, Thailand

Togo—Direction Generale des Postes et Telecommunications, Direction des Services Postaux et Financiers, Loame, Togo

Tokelau—Post Office, Philatelic Bureau, Private Bag, Wanganui, New Zealand

Transkei—Philatelic Services and INTERSAPA, GPO Pretoria 0001, Republic of South Africa

Tristan de Cunha—Postmaster, Jamestown, St. Helena, South Atlantic

Tunisia—Service Philatelique des PTT Bureau, Directeur de Tunis Recette Principale, Tunis, Tunisia

Turkey—Direction Generale des PTT, Department des Postes,

Section de Timbres, Poste, Ankara, Turkey

Turks and Caicos Islands—Philatelic Bureau, Grand Turk, Turks and Caicos Islands, West Indies

Tuvalu—Tuvalu Philatelic Bureau, Funafuti, Tuvalu, Central Pacific

Uganda—Uganda Postes and Telecommunications Corp., Department of Postes, Stamp Bureau, Post Office Box 7159, Kampala, Uganda

Union of Soviet Social Republics—Philatelic Department, V/0 Muzhdunarodnaya Kniga, Moscow 121200, USSR

United Nations—United Nations Postal Administration, Post Office Box 5900, New York, New York 10017

United Nations Postal Administration, Palais des Nations, CH-1211, Geneva 10, Switzerland

United Nations Postal Administration, Vienna International Centre, A-1400, Vienna, Austria

United States of America—U.S. Postal Service, Philatelic Sales Branch, Washington, D.C., 20265, USA

Uruguay—Dirección Nacional de Correos, Oficina Filatelica, Casilla de Correo 1296, Montevideo, Uruguay

Vatican City—Ufficio, Filatelico, Governatorato, Vatican City

Vanda—Philatelic Services and INTERSAP, GPO, Pretoria 0001, Republic of South Africa

Western Samoa—Supervisor, Philatelic Bureau, GPO, Apia, Western Samoa, South Pacific

Yemen-Arab Republic—Ministry of Communications, Philatelic Bureau, GPO, Yemen Republic

People's Democratic Republic of Yemen—Director General of Postes & Telegraphs, GPO, Aden, People's Democratic Republic of Yemen

Yugoslavia—Jugomark, Palmoticeva 2, Belgrade, Yugoslavia

Zambia—Philatelic Bureau, Post Office Box 1857, Ndola, Zambia

Zimbabwe (Rhodesia)—Philatelic Bureau, Post Office Box 4220 Salisbury, Zimbabwe

Glossary

Aniline—water-soluble inks made from a coal-tar base. Because they wash off, they are used so that stamps can not be reused by erasing cancellation marks.

Batonne—a type of paper used for the printing of some stamps. It is thin and lined, quite distinctive from issues regularly available from your post office today.

Bisect—a stamp cut in two. Some stamps are actually perforated for separation in this manner. Others are simply cut by the user. The result is that each half is considered half the postage of the stamp's face amount. Sometimes bisects are authorized by the issuing Post Office, a situation most obvious when perforation marks have been made in the stamp. At other times a bisect has been used and accepted out of necessity due to a shortage of stamps of the necessary value. Collectors seldom collect bisects by themselves. Instead, they collect them on the envelope ("cover") or other mailing device.

Bishop mark—a term related to the stamps of England. Henry Bishop began marking stamps with the month and day that a letter was received in the Post Office sometime around 1861. Many collectors consider the Bishop Marks on England's stamps to be the earliest regular postmarks.

Black jack—not a term related to your knowledge of stamps for investment but rather a general term for a series of United States 2-cent stamps. These black stamps, issued in a number of varieties between 1863 and 1875, feature the profile of Andrew Jackson (Scott type A32). These are among the most popular of early American stamps and entire books have been written about the varieties. Some are quite rare and many will fall into the investment category. However, the term simply refers to all of these stamps and not just one particular year.

Blind perforation—The printing process has pins which poke perforation holes between the stamps. The force of the press and other factors can effect the success or failure of this operation. A totally imperforate sheet or roll of stamps is one of the more valued errors. Less valuable, because it is more common, are blind perforations. A definite impression is made between the stamps but there is not enough force to truly puncture the paper. Even with the lightest blind perforation, a close inspection of the area around the image on the stamp will reveal the marks from the machine.

Block—usually four stamps, two both vertically and horizontally. A block of four will be two stamps high and two stamps wide. These are uncut. A block may include different designs and may have six or more stamps. Generally blocks of four sell for only the price of four of the individual stamps. It is only with *plate blocks* and similar issues that there is a premium over the value of the individual stamps.

Bond paper—an unusually high-quality paper used for some earlier stamps.

Booklets—convenient devices for holding small quantities of stamps. It is most commonly found in vending machines, but owes its origin to 1895 when Luxembourg issued the first such device. One or more blocks or panes are stapled between cardboard covers for protection.

Bourse—a sales area where stamp dealers and collectors gather for buying and selling stamps. Philatelic conventions and many stamp clubs have bourse areas in addition to regular meetings, special auctions, and educational exhibits.

Bull's eyes—cancellation marks perfectly centered on the stamps. Some collectors pay a premium for this type of cancellation on a used stamp. These provide the easiest way to tell the date and city of mailing.

Burelage, burele—a device meant to foil cheaters. It is a special design placed either on the front or back of the stamp to increase the difficulty of erasing a cancellation mark for reuse of the stamp and to reduce the chance of counterfeiting. However, it has been found that if the design is extremely elaborate, counterfeiters actually have an easier time. Handlers become so accustomed to a complex design that they do not study it closely and a counterfeit that is not quite perfect may avoid detection.

Cachet—a design printed, stamped, or hand-drawn on an envelope. It is meant to relate to a particular event or commemoration shown by the stamp. Many First Day Covers are cacheted with the drawing on the envelope directly related to the event for which the postage stamp was issued.

Canceled to order—These are sheets of stamps that have been canceled by the government and sold as "used" for less than the same stamps without the cancellation mark. They have not gone through the mail and are otherwise perfect. They are considered a marketing tool of a government and should be avoided.

Catalog value—the values found in stamp catalogs, such as those issued by Scott and Minkus. They are not "true" values since most dealers feel that the majority of stamps in the catalogs are priced higher than the real market value. Stamps that are extremely rare and in great demand are usually worth more than their catalog value. In addition, variations in the quality of the printing will effect the true selling price of a stamp. Catalog values are best used by comparing the differences over the years. This gives you an idea of relative price increases.

Censored mail—any envelopes which have been labeled, stamped, or hand-marked to indicate the contents have been read before going to the person to whom the letter is addressed. Censorship routinely takes place in many prisons and during wartimes.

Centering—Stamps have margins. Centering determines the relationship of the design to these margins. The more exact the centering, the higher the quality of the stamp in the eyes of a collector. Likewise, when a stamp is badly off center, such as when the perforations run partway through the design, a premium might be paid for the radical error.

Chalky paper—one in a number of devices to foil stamp reuse and counterfeiting. The paper, first used in 1902, can not be erased or washed without the design coming off.

Changeling—Printing errors and inking differences create legitimate variations in stamp colors which affect their desirability among investors. However, some stamps have their color altered by contact with outside substances, chemicals, etc. These stamps may actually lose part of their desirability because the color change came from a cause other than the printing process. Such a stamp is known as a changeling.

Charity seals—These are Easter Sale Seals and any other stamp-like seals issued by charities. Though not stamps, some collectors save them. They are often placed on envelopes but only with proper postage affixed in a corner of the envelope.

Classic—This is a rather loose term such as "antique." Such stamps may or may not be rare. However, a modern stamp which is considered scarce and much in demand is often called a "modern classic" by dealers trying to unload them. This term is quickly dropped if the value of the stamp declines.

Coils—Certain vending machines and machines using stamps instead of a postage marking require stamps in rolls. These have perforation marks between the stamps but usually are smooth on the other two sides. They are always designed so that they are obviously different from those sold in sheets, though seldom is any different value affixed to them.

Combination cover—any envelope with two distinctly different stamps affixed for a special purpose. For example, a letter mailed through two different countries might have to have a stamp from each for some reason. This is a combination cover. Sometimes First Day Covers have two stamps on them. Recently it has been possible to place two related stamps on a cover, having each post-marked on a separate day. Many collectors like to make these covers with stamps from two related areas released on different days. Thus a cover might have a stamp commemorating the anniversary of the birth of a country's leader and a second stamp, again canceled during the First Day of Issue, commemorating the anniversary of that leader's taking power, death or some other important event. If the two topics fall several months apart, two entirely different postage rates might have to be used in addition to the design variations.

Commatology—the collecting of postmarks.

Cover—technically, anything used to hold or "cover" the item being mailed. However, First Day Covers are usually envelopes meant for sending letters. Actually it could mean the First Day cancellation on stamps found on wrapping paper used to send a package.

Crash Cover—a cover recovered from any crashed carrier of the mail. Most collectors think of crash covers coming from mail salvaged after airplanes and/or dirigibles have crashed. Technically mail saved from a train, car, or truck crash could be considered crash covers.

Crease—the fold in a postage stamp. Creases are not natural, though some errors caused by creasing during the printing process are in demand. Creases, other than those which are considered errors, reduce the value of a stamp. The crease weakens the paper and close scrutiny of a stamp can reveal whether or not a collector has moistened, then ironed a creased stamp in an effort to maintain the value of a similiar stamp without the crease.

Cut cancellation—a cancellation which physically cuts the stamp. It was an early experiment to find ways to prevent stamps from being reused.

Cut square—Many collectors like postal stationery: envelopes prepared by the Post Office and sold with postage preprinted. Some collectors ignore the envelopes but cut the postage section and mount it in their albums. The cut is usually rectangular in shape and thus the term "cut square."

Cut to shape—see *Cut square*. This is a similar situation only the cut has been made in the same shape as the postage mark. A circular device detailing the postage will be cut in a circular shape rather than a square cut around the outside.

Dead country—any country whose name has changed or has stopped issuing stamps. Such a term may be applied to a country that has become part of another country through wars or political action, the newly formed nation having a different name.

Definitives—stamps meant for use for several years or at least an unspecified period of time. Commemoratives are generally issued for a set period of time, then new issues come out. A definitive has an unknown life and is usually a regular issue.

Denomination—the value of a stamp as printed on that stamp.

Die—During the printing process, a stamp design is created. Then the design is transferred to a die and the die is used to make the printing plates. The printing plates made in this way will make consistent impressions. Should a die become defective before the plates are finished or should there be need for a new die of the same design, it is likely that there will be subtle differences. The die varieties which result in slight differences in the printing are quite popular with collectors. The Black Jacks, for example, have numerous die varieties, some of which command substantial premiums.

Directory markings—stamps on envelopes or other covers, though usually not over the stamps, which indicate some problem with the delivery of the item. "Moved—No Forwarding Address" stamps on an envelope would be an example of a directory marking.

Duck stamps—stamps depicting ducks (a different design is used annually), which are placed on United States Hunting Permits. These are not postal issues but are extremely popular with investors and collectors. Almost as popular with investors are the large prints made to match the original paintings used for the duck stamps when these are signed by the artist. The original painting chosen for the new duck stamp will eventually command many thousands of dollars from collectors.

Duplex Cancel—This occurs when there are two distinct cancellations. One will have the regular cancellation. The other has the postmark.

Duplicates—a second, third, or more copy of stamps in your collection. However, because there can be subtle printing variations, it is always wise to closely examine duplicates to see if you can detect any differences.

Embossing—a print process called embossing which raises the design (run your finger over the stamp or over stationery). It has been used for making postage stamps but is most common with the making of stationery by the Post Office. The embossed area is the postage.

Entire—Many collectors of stamps will cut out the postage area of an envelope (See *cut square*). When the entire envelope is saved, the item is called an "entire." Some collectors also use this term in reference to covers or mailed envelopes.

Essay—a trial for a new stamp or other postal item design. The essay is created, then rejected by the authorities. Essays are different from counterfeits or created "Cinderella" items in that they were officially made. A decision was made to not use them.

Europa—a term, used since 1956, for the United European nations such as the Common Market countries. Because these issues are popular, countries with no connection with the United Europe concept often issue Europa commemoratives as a way of raising extra money.

Expertizing—a fancy way of saying that a stamp is being checked by experts to see if it is genuine.

Exploded—booklets of stamps, such as those sold in vending machines, when the staple has been removed and all the component parts have been separated are called "exploded."

Fake—This term is different from counterfeits and Cinderellas, which are either created stamps with design unrelated to any in existence (Cinderellas) or forgeries of existing stamps. A fake starts with a genuine stamp, then is altered in some way to make it more desirable. It might have gum added or the value and/or color might have been changed.

Fast colors—stamps made from inks resistant to fading.

First Day Covers—envelopes (covers) with a stamp that has been canceled on the First Day of Issue. Normally only one or a small handful of post offices will provide the distinct First Day of Issue marking.

Flat plate—a printing process. In this case, what is known as a flat-bed plate is used. The common alternative is the use of a cylindrical plate. This is a technical term seldom encountered in terms of investment rarity.

Forerunners—stamps used in an area which, years later, takes on a different name. The most common example usually cited are the stamps of Israel. Stamps from Turkey postally canceled before 1918 in Palestine were actually canceled in the area which later became Israel. Other issues fall into this category as well, though these facts are more collector curiosities than items which seriously effect the value. However, should a collector of a country such as Israel also want to put together a series of forerunners, the historical value of the collection can be great. Collectors exhibiting at stamp shows often consider such an approach because an unusually interesting display is possible at often reasonable expense.

Forgery—a reproduction of a genuine postage stamp. It is meant either to be used as regular postage, thus defrauding the government and cutting mailing costs, or it is meant to mislead a collector. In the latter incident, the collector will spend money for a rarity that proves to be a fraud. This term is distinctly different from the term "fake" as defined in philately.

Frame—the outer area of a stamp's design.

Frank—a marking somewhere on the envelope or cover indicating that the item must travel without charge through the mail. Many elected officials have a franking privilege. Benjamin Franklin, when working for the British postal system, used to sign his covers "Free, B. Franklin." Some franks have been stamped on the mail and others are handwritten. Some collectors enjoy obtaining covers from various government officials, soldiers who may have had this privilege in wartime, and others.

Freak—a genuine stamp gone a little strange because of one or more unexpected circumstances. For example, a small section of paper may have become folded during the printing process, altering the design or the perforations. These circumstances are usually unique, affecting one stamp or section of a sheet, instead of several sheets, as might occur with a printing error.

Front—half of a cover and thus a step up from the cut square. Some collectors do not take the cut square but rather that half of the cover which contains all postal information, including the address, addressee, stamp and cancellation. This is far less desirable than retaining the entire cover, even when the letter mailed in the cover is long gone.

Fugitive inks—water-soluble inks that run easily. Their use in printing postage stamps is to ensure difficulty for those who might counterfeit or alter the stamps.

Goldbeater's skin—the nineteenth century was filled with numerous ways to try and foil counterfeiters. One of the oddest was devised by Prussia in 1886. The idea was to utilize a paper that was so unusual that, when printed and gum applied, removal would be impossible. The paper was translucent so that the gum could be applied over the printing and still be read. Once the stamp was attached to the envelope, any attempt to remove the stamp also resulted in its destruction.

Grill—there are several different uses for this type of concept, originating with counterfeiting difficulties in the nineteenth century. The addition of a grill by first the United States and then Peru was actually an embossing tool. There are also grill designs simply used for cancelling stamps, though these are quite different. All grills are patterns which form a grid. These might be parallel lines or dots indicating the ends of where such lines would be if they were actually used.

Gum—the general term for all adhesive applied to the backs of postage stamps so they can be placed in albums.

Gutter—the margin, which is usually unprinted, that is found between the panes of stamps on a sheet.

Handstamp—the cancellation applied by hand to a stamp. Prior to more complete automation of the mail, letters that contained somewhat fragile items were marked for handstamping, though this was often rougher than with the early canceling machines. During the early days of the postal service, handstamping was common and often postmasters would design their own unique stamps.

Hinge—a small, gummed piece of paper meant to attach stamps to albums. These are peelable when dry but any trace of hinging on a stamp that otherwise had full gum may have less appeal to collectors and might lower its selling price.

Imperforate—The earliest stamps were issued in such a way that they had to be separated by cutting. Then stamps were perforated so that they could be easily separated by hand. Almost all stamps since 1860 have had perforations. When modern stamps go through the printing process without being perforated or having an indication that perforations were attempted (see *"Blind" perforation*), this is usually an error valued by collectors. There are occasionally deliberately imperforate stamps sold by modern postal authorities, but these are not considered rarities even when the number printed are deliberately kept low to "justify" an initially high selling price.

India paper—This is one paper not used to foil counterfeiting. It is thin but of high quality, primarily used for trial impressions from the die or printing plate. Such trials are known as proofs (q.v.).

Intaglio—a type of printing, usually line engraving or photogravure. The impression is made by the section of the printing plate that is recessed.

Kiloware—The purchase of stamp packets was mentioned earlier. Countries using the metric system often have packets prepared by weight. A large quantity is sold by the kilogram, which is 2.3 pounds. Kiloware refers to this type of stamp sale and you can be fairly certain that valuable stamps are not likely to be found in such purchases.

Labels—stickers similar in appearance to stamps but not postal issues. An Easter Seal or similar item would technically fit this term.

Laid paper—There are two types of paper most commonly used for printing stamps. One is "laid" paper and the other is "wove" paper. Hold the paper to the light and examine it. Laid paper will have thin parallel lines visible. Wove paper is evenly textured. Laid paper is less commonly used than wove paper, but neither affects the value of a stamp.

Letterpress—a type of printing that involves inking from the raised surface of the plate instead of the recessed surface as is found with Intaglio printing.

Line engraving—a hand-engraved die used to date an intaglio printing will result in a line engraving.

Line pair—When ink collects between two dies, the subsequent printing will yield a visible line. This is usually called a joint die line or guide line. A pair of stamps with what are known as joint die line pairs usually sells for a premium over the ordinary pairs of stamps found in a coil.

Lithography—a type of printing where the design is meant to hold ink and the section without a design repels it during the printing.

Locals—postage stamps whose use is confined to a limited area. A postmaster might produce a local stamp for a particular city, but additional stamps would be needed to go elsewhere in the country. Such local issues have been produced at various times in many countries.

Margin—The most common use of this term is in reference to the unprinted area surrounding the design. As has been seen, the more even the margin surrounding the design, the more collectors prize the stamp, all other factors being equal. A second definition refers to a sheet of stamps, the margin being that area surrounding the printed stamps, an area also known as selvage. In this case, the margin may have printing rather than being free of any inscription, numbers or other markings.

Maximum card—a postcard which has a photograph or drawing that is related directly to the design of the stamp. Usually there is a postal cancellation that is tied to the same theme.

Metered mail—a device for applying postage prepaid postmarks without using stamps. It is government authorized. Once the mail has been imprinted with this information, the letter or parcel can be sent through the mail. The metered mail is usually used by large-volume mailers who have their meters set in advance by the Post Office. Such metered mail has been acceptable to the Universal Postal Union since 1920.

Miniature sheets—smaller-than-normal sheets of postage stamps often issued as profit-making items for sale to collectors.

Mint—the condition of a stamp as it comes off the press. It will be unused, without damage, and have full gum if gum was used with the stamp. The quality of the printing, the positioning of the design in relation to the margin, whether or not an error was made are all factors in the eventual value to a collector. But any stamp which is in the original condition it was issued from the Post Office is a "mint" stamp.

Missionary mixture—Missions and other institutions raise money by clipping the stamps from envelopes and packages they receive. They then put together a mixture for resale either directly or through dealers. Many duplicates are likely to be found, and it is the rare exception when an item of value is included.

Missionaries—a term applied to the 1851–1852 postal issues of Hawaii. They are greatly in demand.

Mixed perforation—Stamps have perforations either on two or four sides. When the spacing and/or size do not match, as determined by a perforation gauge, you have a mixed perforation.

Mixed postage—an envelope or cover that has the postage stamps from two or more areas, each issuing its own postage. The need for this postage in order for the cover to have gone through the mail is essential if this term is to be applied.

Mobile post office—a term for portable mail-handling equipment. During the years when trains were the major method of transportation, postal cars might be attached and these would be considered part of a mobile post office.

Multiple—two or more stamps attached together as issued, though less than a full sheet or roll.

Native paper—a reference to the type of paper used for some stamps. This was a cost or convenience factor, not a method for attempting to foil counterfeiters. The paper is usually crude and made locally in the area where used.

New issue service—an aspect of many dealers' retail operations. The dealers arrange for the purchase of new issues for the various clients desiring them. You send a deposit and issues are provided to the limits of the deposit. Occasionally a collector using such a service is able to obtain what becomes a modern rarity. However, such a situation occurs so rarely that investors avoid these services except for the hobby part of their philatelic enjoyment.

Newspaper stamps—Over the years there were stamps issued specifically for the prepayment of newspapers and other printed materials. The collection of these stamps has become a popular aspect of stamp collecting for some individuals.

Obliteration—a method of cancellation which is so thorough that it is impossible to reuse the stamps. This type of cancellation mark is often called a "killer." However, the term obliteration is sometimes applied to only the partial destruction of a stamp.

Obsolete—a stamp that can be used to send letters through the mail. However, it is no longer sold at the post office, usually because a new issue has taken its place.

Occupation issue—stamps reflecting wartime or periods of political upheaval. They are issued for use during a period when a country is occupied by others.

Off center—When a stamp is not centered. This is not an error but rather a normal problem with the printing of stamps. Off-center stamps are less desirable than well-centered stamps.

Officials—stamps issued for use by government employees for special purposes within the bureaucracy. They may or may not be sold through the Post Office.

Offset—a term used to reflect a problem with the design transfer caused by ink which has not dried. A sheet of stamps is printed, the ink is still wet, and a second sheet is laid over the first. The design from the wet sheet is transferred to the back of the sheet on top. This results in a mirror image and such an impression does not add to the value of the sheet. It is only when stamps are deliberately printed on both sides that the value is altered. These are printing errors so extreme that the stamps command a premium with collectors.

OHMS—a device added to British Commonwealth postage to indicate that it is being given official use. It stands for On His/Her Majesty's Service.

Omnibus issue—a general term relating to a period when several countries release stamps relating to a common theme, such as an international sporting event, the anniversary of Queen Elizabeth's reign, the marriage of Prince Charles and Lady Diana or numerous others. Sometimes there is a common design element among the issuing countries, but other times this is not a consideration.

On-paper—stamps that still have some of the original envelope attached. The missionary mixtures mentioned earlier usually fit this category. The stamps are cut or torn from envelopes with a portion of the envelope remaining. This is different from what is known as "on piece," which also involves stamps on paper. However, in these cases, the paper is necessary to prove the authenticity of the stamp. For example, a bisect will have enough paper to show the cancellation mark and prove that it is genuine, not just a stamp the collector cut in half after receiving it.

Original gum—the adhesive that existed when the stamp came from the Post Office. Stamps can be regummed when the adhesive has been removed and prior to 1890, most people soaked off the gum of stamps they collected. The earlier a stamp was issued, the less likely it is to have the original gum.

Overprint—any printing that is placed over the original design of the stamp. The term "surcharge" is used if the overprinting is meant to increase the cost of the postage, a measure sometimes used when rates are increased.

Oxidation—a term used to explain changes in color of stamps. It refers to the altering of inks that appear to oxidize or rust, such as an orange ink used on a stamp which, over time, changes to brown. This change does not increase the value of a stamp and may drastically reduce what a collector or dealer will pay.

Packet letter—letters carried by ships which are authorized to carry mail. They are often government owned vessels.

Pair—two unseparated stamps which generally are valued at double the price of the single stamp. There is generally no special premium just because there are two together.

Pane—a term for the sheet of stamps sold at post offices. Technically a sheet of stamps is the size sheet created by the printer. These large sheets are then cut down, usually into four equal parts, and shipped to post offices for sale. Each of these sheets for sale at the post office is called a pane. Thus, technically, the modern sales vehicle has four panes per sheet of stamps when you purchase the stamps. When stamps are divided further and formed into booklets for vending machines and other sales, each stamp "page" of the booklet is also called a pane or booklet pane.

Paquebot—a special cancellation to indicate that mailing was done on board a ship.

Parcel post stamps—stamps found in many countries to indicate that an item was mailed with parcel post fees paid.

Pelure paper—a paper that looks something like onion skin and has been used at times for the production of stamps. It has the advantages of being strong and thin.

Penny Black—Generally considered the first postage stamp as we know them today. It bears the image of Queen Victoria and was first issued on May 6, 1840.

Perfins—another control device that has been used over the years to foil those who would steal stamps. It is a stamp which has been perforated or punched with a design or other marking. These have been made both privately and for public use.

Perforation—the holes punched around the stamps on a sheet to allow them to be easily torn out. However, there are different types of perforations, all meant to serve the same purpose. A *harrow* perforation occurs when a sheet of stamps has all the holes punched at once. If only three sides are punched for a row, then the process repeated over and over again until the sheet has been fully perforated, this is known as a *comb* perforation. When the holes are punched a row at a time, you have a process known as *line* perforation, which often results in unevenness of marking on a sheet.

Perforation gauge—The way the perforation holes are made can indicate different printings of a particular stamp. In order to know whether or not a stamp might be scarcer in one type of printing than another, it is necessary to use a scale or gauge that measures the number of perforation holes in a 2-centimeter distance. These are generally inexpensive items made from paper, cardboard, metal, and other substances that are as easy to use as a ruler.

Permit—Large-volume mailers using fourth-class postage can buy a permit that is assigned a particular number. The mailer places this permit number on the mail rather than using postage stamps.

Phantoms—bogus stamps of one sort or another. They may be counterfeits or, more likely, stamps issued for countries that do not exist. You will also see words such as "Fantasy," "Phantasy," and "Cinderellas" applied to such items.

Phosphor—a substance that reacts to ultraviolet light. Great Britain started using lines of phosphor in order to print stamps back in 1959 and numerous other countries have adopted phosphor in their printing techniques. It is a common tool among countries involved with automatic mail handling.

Photogravure—an approach to the production of stamps. It starts with a designer's original drawing being photographed. Then a plate is made with the design impressed in the surface, ink applied so that it rests in the depressions, the remaining ink being wiped from the otherwise smooth plate. The paper reproduces the design because of the ink that is in the grooves of the design in the plate.

Plate—the basic tool of the printing system because it is the item placed on the press. American stamps have identifying numbers for each plate used and these numbers, accompanied by a block of stamps, form the collectible known as the "plate number block."

Plate number block—a block of stamps with that portion of the margin bearing the plate number (see *Plate*).

Plating—a form of collecting in which stamps of a design are collected so that, when put together, they re-create the original sheet. This is usually done with older issues.

Plebiscite issue—are stamps related to countries whose status was in question immediately after World War I. The League of Nations acted as temporary administrator for countries that were scheduled to vote on whether they would be independent nations or join with other countries. The stamps issued by such areas as Schleswig, Allenstein, and Upper Silesia, among numerous others, fall into this category.

PNC—a term for philatelic/numismatic cover. These are usually First Day Covers that include a coin or medal related to the event being commemorated. The relationship of the stamp and coin or medal are what make the PNC. Usually these are issued privately but some, such as those related to the 1976 U.S. Bicentennial, have been issued by the Post Office and the Mint.

Pneumatic post—an unusual form of mailing in which pneumatic tubes are used for the delivery of mail. France and Italy are the major users of the pneumatic post and Italy has periodically issued stamps for this particular type of system.

Postage dues—stamps that indicate the difference between the postage paid, if any, on a piece of mail and the amount to be collected. The money owed is usually collected upon delivery.

Postal card—different from a postcard, though it is the same general size. A postcard usually has a picture on one side and a space for writing a message on the other. There is a place for a stamp but postage has not been affixed. A postal card, on the other hand, is an official card with preprinted postage. The card and postage are paid for at the time the item is obtained from the post office.

Postal history—a general term which does not directly reflect an investor's concern. It refers to the study of the postal routes, markings, general development of the system, and other matters similar to what was covered in the first chapter of this book. However, postal history material has become a popular collectible and the items often rise in value when sold at auctions.

Postal stationery—like postal cards. It is stationery with preprinted postage instead of postage stamps. Envelopes, aerograms, and similar items fall into this category provided the postage is printed in advance, not added with an adhesive postage stamp.

Postally used—an item that has been used for mailing.

Precancels—When large mailings are required by a company, machine-printed cancellations may be applied at the post office. A business with a special permit can buy precanceled stamps to apply to speed handling. A precancel issued from a community post office is known as a "Local" and one applied in Washington, D.C., by the Bureau of Engraving and Printing is known as a "Bureau."

Pre-stamp covers—highly prized collectibles that are envelopes and other covers used to move the mail before postage stamps were used.

Printer's waste—stamps misprinted so badly that inspectors should have pulled them and destroyed them. Occasionally a printing firm will dispose of this waste through special dump sites and these items have been taken, then sold as errors. Some sell as though they were rarities and others are discredited and destroyed. Although printer's waste does enter the market fairly regularly, these items should be avoided.

Pro Juventute—semi-postal issues issued by the Swiss, a portion of the revenue being given to various child welfare organizations.

Proofs—trial impressions from the die or printing plate which are made before the production of the stamps. A proof allows the printer to check the design, color, inking, and other factors. Proofs are quite scarce in the open market but little enough known that they are frequently underpriced for their rarity.

Provisional—a postage stamp used when demands for stamps temporarily exceed supplies. They are not regular issues and have been issued by local postmasters.

Receiving mark—a post office marking made by the office receiving a letter or package when normally postmarks are applied only when sending the items.

Redrawn—a stamp design which is a minor change or correction from the original design.

Regionals—a term primarily reserved for Great Britain's special issues since 1958. Stamps were issued for such regions as Northern Ireland, Wales, the Isle of Man, Jersey, and Guernsey, the stamps being valid only for sale in that region. Such stamps could not be used anywhere else in Great Britain but regionals could be sent from the appropriate area throughout Great Britain. Thus an Isle of Man stamp could be used to mail a letter to Jersey, but that same stamp could not be used to carry a letter from Jersey to the Isle of Man. That would require a Jersey stamp specifically.

Registered mail—a form of first-class mail which includes a numbered receipt. The value of the item is noted and there is insurance paid if it is lost. The registered mail item requires individual post office employees to sign as they handle something for closer control of the item mailed.

Registration labels—part of the registered mail process, labels, which note the registered item's number and, usually, the city from which it originated.

Remainders—stocks of stamps that have not been sold by the post office at the time that the design is declared obsolete. All countries have remainders but how they handle their elimination will vary. These may be sold at substantial discount over face value, either unmarked, exactly as they were when still in regular sale, or with a special cancellation mark.

Repaired stamps—stamps that have been damaged in some way, then repaired to increase their desirability. Sometimes this is done just to improve a stamp that otherwise might be falling apart. Other times this is done to commit fraud on an unsuspecting buyer.

Replicas—In the early days of stamp collecting, some companies printed copies of rare or unusual stamps to serve as space fillers. These were not meant to be exact duplicates and were usually printed in a single color. They are so obviously wrong that there never has been a concern about them being counterfeits.

Reprint—a stamp printed from the original printing plate but after the stamp is officially no longer being made. Sometimes this reprinting is fully legitimate and relates to the government's desire to produce a special presentation piece. The colors of the inking may be altered to further make this a special item. At other times this is done privately and may be meant to fool collectors.

Retouch—a minor repair made in a damaged die or plate to allow it to continue being used for the printing process. A retouch results in a stamp that is slightly different from the original prior to that action being taken. This is quite different from work done on the stamps themselves.

Revenues—Special stamps and labels have been printed over the years for use in indicating the payment of taxes. These have been affixed to documents, merchandise, and other items. Sometimes these are labels and other times they are stamps that can be used for both postage and revenue. There are also revenue issues that, because of a local stamp shortage, were pressed into use as postage. Since this use is a provisional, collectors want to have such revenue labels on the original cover to indicate the unusual use of postage.

Rocket mail—Ever since the first peacetime efforts to find uses for rockets other than hurtling bombs, letters have been sent by rockets as experiments. Often these are specially marked and the collecting of such marked items is known as the collecting of rocket mail.

'Roos—the nickname of the 1913 Australian stamp which featured a kangaroo on the map of Australia. It was the first Australian stamp design with variations used for the next thirty-two years, among others.

Rouletting—You will notice a series of dashes on a stamp that has been rouletted. The action of rouletting involves piercing the paper between stamps to make their separation easier. This does not puncture the surface of the paper, however.

Rust—a deep brown mold known to form on stamps stored in tropical humidity areas. It decreases the resale value of your stamp.

Selvage—the margin area on a sheet or pane of stamps; it is not printed.

Series—a particular issue of stamps collected for all the variations in design and value.

Se-Tenant—two or more stamps of different designs, types, colors and/or denominations that are joined together.

Shade—Stamps may have minor variations in the basic color because of differences in the inking over time. These variations do not effect the value unless they are unusually different.

Sheet—the complete set of stamps on one large page as printed. Each sheet is cut into panes (see *Pane*) for sale at the Post Office.

Ship letter—a letter carried by a private ship and different from a *packet letter*.

Short set—a partial series with the higher values usually being the ones that are missing. A common sales term.

Soaking—a method of removing stamps from the paper to which they are attached. Details of how to do this are in Chapter 4. In some instances, soaking will destroy the stamps because the inks are not color fast in water.

Souvenir card—a card issued by the postal service in conjunction with some event. It is a philatelic issue but can not be used as postage.

Souvenir sheet—a small sheet of stamps with a special commemorative description. The stamps shown may be only one value or offset by extremely wide margins. Often these can be used to mail letters but the purpose is to appeal to collectors.

Space filler—a stamp in rotten condition which is used to fill a space. Usually space fillers are purchased when a stamp is a high-priced rarity in better conditions and the extremely worn, battered examples are within your budget. Everyone who buys space fillers usually hopes to better the example through a future purchase when budget allows.

Special delivery—a stamp that indicates that unusually fast service is being provided.

Specimens—Postal organizations belonging to the Universal Postal Union often will issue examples of forthcoming stamps to the hobby press and others. This provides advance publicity. However, the stamps are not to be used and have the word "Specimen" overprinted. The collecting of specimens is growing in popularity, though they seldom achieve the value of proofs.

Straight edge—When a sheet of stamps has strips of stamps along the edge without perforations, there will be one or two sides per stamp that are imperforate. These are known as straight edges and may be marked with a colored line.

Strip—a row of three or more unseparated stamps.

Surcharge—an overprint with a new denomination for the stamp. A surcharge is often added when stamps are prepared at one value, then the value is raised and there is no time to reprint with the new figure.

Surface colored paper—paper used for printing on which one side is white and the other side is some other color.

Sweatbox—one of a number of devices meant to unstick stamps which have adhered to one another. The idea is to separate them without damaging the gum.

"T" or Taxe—The single letter "T" has been used in France to indicate that a stamp was actually postage due. The French postal authorities generally follow a pattern of stamping the letter T (or hand marking it) on a stamp when postage due has been paid with the stamp and using the T on the envelope or other cover when postage due is to be paid.

Telegraph stamps—labels to indicate the payment of telegraph fees.

Tête-bêche—a slightly odd arrangement of stamps involving two or more which are attached together but one of which is upside down in relation to the other. The term comes from a French term meaning "head to tail."

Tied—a term used when you have a cover on which the cancellation mark is on both the stamp and the envelope or other wrapper.

Topical—a stamp whose design fits a collectible theme such as athletic events, airplanes, birds, flowers, etc.

Transit mark—a mark made on a stamp or cover by a post office other than the one from which the package was mailed and the one to which it is being sent. It is an interim marking.

Triptych—Three stamps, all joined together, which have either a common theme or which, together, form a single design.

Type—a specific design.

Underprint—a design, under the basic design of the stamp, making it difficult to duplicate.

Ungummed—while this may mean a stamp which has had its gum removed, many countries have issued stamps without gum at one time or another. This term also refers to such designs.

Unhinged—This is a term to watch carefully. It is different from "mint, never hinged" discussed earlier in that it only means that there are no hinge marks visible on the stamp. Such a term can be applied to a stamp on which the gum was removed, then new gum applied. Only a mint stamp must have the original gum, yet both a mint and a regummed stamp can be called unhinged.

Unused—An unused stamp has no cancellation marks. However, the gum might be removed and the stamp might have gone through the mail without being canceled. This is an ambiguous term much like unhinged—only it should be more specific.

Used—Any stamp that has been canceled, regardless of condition.

Variety—Any stamp which differs from the original design through a change in color, the accidental imperforation or the perforation of an issue which should have been perforated, or some similar deviation from the standard design issue.

Vignette—a specific design created so that there is shading. The basic design slowly blends into the surrounding area making printing easier. When there are specific lines around the design, minor problems with the printing are instantly noticed.

Watermark—a manufacturing process that creates a thinning of the paper so that a semi-translucent pattern can be seen either through special filtered light or the use of pure benzine and a black tray. There is a variation of watermark manufacture that creates a thickening of the paper, such as on some Romanian stamps. The latter are known as positive watermarks, while the former are negative watermarks. Special detectors must be used with caution because while the traditional use of benzine is harmless for most stamps, it can cause the ink to run on others (Early Czechoslovak stamps, in some instances).

Wing margin—Sheets of stamps printed in Britain before 1880 often had a distinct margin. Perforations were down the center of the gutter so that there were oversized margins on one side of the stamp.

Wove paper—The paper most commonly used in stamp production today. It is noted for its evenness because the process results in a uniform texture.

Wrapper—a flat sheet of paper, open at both ends, used to wrap a newspaper, magazine, or similar periodical. In the past, such wrappers had values imprinted on them.

Zemstvos—stamps issued by the Russian municipal governments during the ruling of the Czar. They were authorized in 1870 and are often quite scarce because of their limited use.

Zeppelin issues—A Zeppelin, dirigible, or blimp, all interchangeable terms, were often honored by special stamps or covers carried on these flights.

Index